T0116449

BEAUTIFUL
ARE THE FEET

Memories of Marathons:
Walking and performing Mark's gospel as solo theatre.

Geoffrey Darling

WESTBOW
PRESS®
A DIVISION OF THOMAS NELSON
& ZONDERVAN

WestBow Press books may be ordered through booksellers or by contacting:

WestBow Press
A Division of Thomas Nelson & Zondervan
1663 Liberty Drive
Bloomington, IN 47403
www.westbowpress.com
844-714-3454

Scripture quotations marked (KJV) are taken from
King James version of the Bible, public domain.

ISBN: 979-8-3850-1398-2 (sc)
ISBN: 979-8-3850-1399-9 (e)

Library of Congress Control Number: 2023923434

Print information available on the last page.

WestBow Press rev. date: 12/15/2023

How beautiful upon the mountains are the feet of him that bringeth good tidings, that publisheth peace; that bringeth good tidings of good, that publisheth salvation; that saith unto Zion, Thy God reigneth!
Isaiah 52:7 (KJV)

To the greater glory of God

Now, in seeking deep insight,
I make a promise to the light.
To keep it always shining bright.
For light within needs light without,
And without light, there is no sight.
Geoffrey Darling

ACKNOWLEDGMENTS

I began this account, of my roughly twenty-five years of performing St Mark's gospel, to create a fundraising tool to accompany future walks, on behalf of charities. Any person who is active, fit, well-preserved, and even in their mid-seventies, should undertake such walks, if time and family circumstances allow. I thank God daily that I can and that all those factors do.

As the tale grew in the telling, it took on many other facets. So, continuing the diamond metaphor, as I revisited and polished the memories of those many years, it focused my faith and like a drink of living water, showed me my greatest need is to serve others, and to let my light so shine before men. Thus, my greatest thanks go to my wife Rose, whose entry into my life is captured in Chapter Seven, to Keith and Jean Ross of Hamilton, whose similar entries come very early in the journey, to the staff at the Bible Society in New Zealand for their loving support, to the late Rev. Dr. James Stuart who sowed the first seeds, to the hosts in every New Zealand city—except Nelson, so far—who have accommodated my journey and hosted presentations, to the Irish pastors, Rev. John Woodside (Drogheda, Co. Meath) and Rev. Canon Chris Matchett (Newtownards, Co. Down) who welcomed me with unqualified acceptance and outstanding hospitality, to the many prison chaplains in Ohio who were equally welcoming, and to every single one of the thousands of people who have come to hear the gospel spoken aloud, as it was in the early days of the Christian church. Those people became my biggest strength.

A special thanks to Craig Bates, owner of Bates Photographix, Hawera, New Zealand, a dedicated servant of Jesus and a long-standing colleague and friend, who generously donated the rights to the striking front cover photograph, taken in the shadow of the 8261ft. Mount Taranaki, in 2004. And to my late father Bruce, whose epitaph is three simple words, "Never Give In."

I also formally acknowledge and thank the following for their permission to reprint other copyright material: A photograph of the author on the march near Timaru, taken in 2002, courtesy of Stuff Ltd., New Zealand. The appendix article by Claire Allison, published by *The Timaru Herald,* June 27, 2002, and reprinted by permission of Stuff Ltd. The appendix article, *Kemra Bank,* is an excerpt from *The Inch* by Alma Rutherford, published by The Clutha Leader Print in 1958, and reprinted by kind permission of the Rutherford family, who generously provided several local names to enhance my story of the walk through their part of South Otago.

PROLOGUE

As I drifted asleep, my body began to shake and vibrate rhythmically. Then a buzzing roar drummed in my head. I felt as if my central core was succumbing to the rapid, rippling waves. Through the noise and confusion came a quiet, still command, "Do Mark."

It was a command of such gentle power, cutting through the chaotic shaking and noise, that I believed I must be hearing the Holy Spirit. On reflection, I was certain. I recall Jesus's disciples experiencing a mighty wind when they encountered the promised "Comforter" for the first time.

This was not my first encounter with what I shall call the astral plane. This name is for the state between sleeping and waking which I experienced a little in my youth but found a bit frightening. I prayed to be rid of it and the half-dreams ceased for many years. So, I was surprised when the once-familiar vibrations began again. And, as I write almost one-quarter century later, I am still surprised but also continually grateful.

These are my adventures and experiences when I obeyed that quiet, still invitation to, "Do Mark." By this command, the words meant the exercise I was currently involved in, the task of learning to perform St. Mark's gospel as solo theatre. This was neither a promise nor a suggestion. It was a command.

I was in my early fifties, an actor, though I earned my daily bread as a journalist and had done so for twenty years. I was driving a long distance to take up a new job as the sole journalist/editor of a small weekly community newspaper in the center of New Zealand's North Island. I was learning Mark's gospel in the Contemporary English Version (CEV) to present at a conference three months in the future.

This was a day of new beginnings, May 1, 2000, a day that included a fourteen-hour drive that I became too tired to complete. I was still one hundred kilometers (sixty miles) short of my goal when I pulled into a rest stop. I snuggled into my comforting sleeping bag and believed I met the Comforter. Ironic? Perhaps, but irony aside, "Do Mark", promised much and you readers, who may have encountered one of my presentations, are the most important part of the journey.

I begin the story in the first month of the new century, when the late Rev. Dr. Jim Stuart, pastor of Wellington's St Andrew's on the Terrace, suggested I perform Mark for a national conference, which our church would be hosting in July, six months ahead. In agreeing, I suppose I was saying "Yes" to "Do Mark", and from that moment my life had a new purpose.

It's no secret that my life was at a low ebb before Jim gave it direction. I thought my journalism career had dried up and "home" was a series of shared roommate situations. Jim took me on faith in my ability, knowing I'd performed a solo piece based on my mother's journey with dementia, at the Wellington Fringe Festival. He told me about a performance he'd seen of Mark's gospel in America, and he suggested I do the same. I accepted the challenge.

CHAPTER ONE

IN STARTING TO create a dramatic presentation of Mark's gospel, I tried to simulate the experience that people of Jesus's time would have had, of hearing the good news for the first time, to continue the oral tradition of storytelling, of hearing and not reading, just as people have experienced for thousands of years, and gained new life in the process. I wanted to continue that tradition and make the stories come alive for my audiences.

I started to learn the 1611 King James Version but soon stumbled and fell over the archaic pronouns, the use of thee and thou, and when I should use which one. An actor friend, Wickham Pack, suggested I look at the Contemporary English Version (CEV), a translation by the American Bible Society. "It's written to be read aloud," she said. I found it flowed very easily.

By May 1, 2000, I had learned about four chapters in three months and had another three months to cement the remaining twelve. That was a slow start, but I was relearning how to learn, and I knew that, as I opened the channels, the conduits as it were, to my memory receptors, the words would stick more rapidly. The more I learned, the easier it became. But I'll leave a lecture on learning-by-rote techniques to another chapter.

As I settled into the new job in Taumarunui, I had the blessing of accommodation at a "dacha" in a small town nearby called Owhango, courtesy of a St. Andrew's, Wellington, elder and his wife, the Hon. Hugh Templeton and Natasha. Of Russian origin, she liked to call their holiday home in Owhango the dacha. I spent three weeks there, thanks to their hospitality, and made great strides in learning.

I joined Christ Church, the small Anglican church in Taumarunui, and shared my mission of learning Mark's gospel with the copastoral team of Val and Lance Riches. They encouraged me, just as I shared my progress with them. I used the church in several quiet evenings to learn, rehearse, and revise. One Sunday morning, Val put me on the spot when the liturgy called for a reading from Mark 6, about John the Baptist and Herod's daughter and her demanding his head on a plate. Val guessed that I must have chapter 6 under my belt by then and, without warning, beckoned me to the front. I walked forward feeling as if my own head was on a platter, but I got through it, though a little shakily, and made sure it was never so unprepared again.

I carried on rehearsing and learning, and Val and Lance at Christ Church offered to let me present the whole gospel a week before the conference in Wellington. The congregation was small but appreciative. How many times have we heard that phrase? One church stalwart, a middle-aged man, was a bit disruptive when he climbed over a couple of parishioners, stomped to the small library at the back to get not just one but three versions of the Bible, and came back to his seat, equally loudly, and rustled through the pages to find where I was and what I had missed out. When we got to the last three chapters of the Passion story, Val and Lance's ten-year-old daughter declared, with youthful glee, that she "liked this bit." And so did I, and her.

Afterward, an assistant priest, or so I assumed him to be since he was robed in white, came back to where I was changing and offered, almost insisted, in a very charming and sincere manner, to help me in any way he could. That was almost a quarter of a century ago, and he still is. Thanks again, Keith Ross.

I kept learning and practicing as winter drew in, and in July, I traveled to Wellington for the conference and performance. It went well enough, but it was obvious to me that I needed some directing, and I accepted the offer of such from a friend who'd come to the opening performance at St. Andrew's on The Terrace, and who thought the same thing, that my performance needed a director's touch. We rehearsed at his home in a neighboring town and with his four-year-old son watching, which produced a treasured early memory. After the little lad had seen the story of Jesus raising Jairus' daughter from a deathlike coma, he got up and started walking around, acting out the story. To this day I cannot reach that uplifting story without seeing the small boy, now a grown man, I imagine, walking with glee and his own creativity. As the years have passed, few passages in Mark's sixteen chapters do *not* have an accompanying memory.

Some were good and others tragic. Jesus calming the storm in Mark 4 always reminds me of four junior boys from our high school who lost their lives on Lake Rotorua. The lake is the same size as Lake Galilee, the same shape and even the same depth, about ninety feet maximum, relatively shallow and easily turned treacherous by a windstorm. The four sea scouts took a small sailing boat onto the lake in question in early spring. A squall hit the boat and it capsized. Two tried to swim the three kilometers (two miles) to shore in a heavy swell and drowned. The two who stayed with the upturned boat died of exposure before they could be rescued. When representing Jesus calming the waters, I invariably think of them. They'd be in their mid-seventies now, as I am.

It would be nice to announce that once the brilliance of the first performance had swept over all who saw it at the conference, the world beat a path to my door as if I'd built a better mousetrap. But nothing worth doing comes that easily, and I waited for my next performances to come from the many letters I sent out.

Meanwhile, I began to grow very fond of Taumarunui and its characters. One of the characteristics of a small and isolated town is how it spawns characters. I had not been long in the town and was still staying at the Templeton dacha when I walked into the local for a postworkday drink. I met a character who told me I'd got the job he wanted. I bought him a drink, which was probably his aim in the first place, and we talked. He said he'd been a professional actor and among his credits was an appearance at Tauranga's Gateway Players about twenty-five years before in *Mothers and Fathers*, written by Joe Musaphia for two men and two women. I had played one of them, a traffic cop, so this must be …? I searched his face for his name and struggled to recognize him, so firmly had the decay of the intervening years set in. The name finally came. "Lionel!"

"Well, actually they call me Larry around here." He was known as Larry for his harmonica playing, a tribute to Larry Adler. The locals called him "Electric Larry" because he'd become an electrician and a bright sparky at that.

I shook my head at the intervening years' cruel damage, sure that he probably thought the same of me. We had another couple of pints, and he invited me to share his house. So accommodation was sorted out, and we settled into a winter of content.

After the first presentation of Mark, I decided I needed a more authentic costume, and I found some suitable brown Lycra cloth and a tailor in Taumarunui willing to make a very presentable version of a Franciscan monk's garb. I have used it in every performance since 2000.

The newspaper and Mark occupied my time, and in the spring I began to plan a tour, by foot, with performances of Mark along the way. I decided that walking from the center of the North Island (Taumarunui) to the top would attract much interest. I needed to get fitter and went on several thirty-kilometer (twenty-mile) walks at weekends. That was the distance I needed to cover each day.

I thought at one stage of skating on in-line skates and bought a pair and could barely master them when a *Waikato Times* reporter Rosemarie North thought me a good fit for a lighthearted story, arranged her photographer to stand fifty meters away with a telephoto lens and let me rip, with large book simulating a Bible under my arm. I traveled twenty meters, barely; he got the shot, and I realized I could not go far on the stone-chip pavement that covered most New Zealand roads. It got in the paper though, but I did not skate a step, even as I passed through its circulation area.

I was not keen on carrying a pack on my back and tried pushing an old pram instead. I persuaded a secondhand dealer to lend me one. And that was what I used to set off with in the spring (September) of 2001, a few days after 9/11. That might seem like a long time between performances, but the previous few months had seen me traveling, often weekly, to venues along the route: I talked to churches, arranged publicity, planned accommodation, and kept both my fingers crossed and my faith alight.

My first day was walking out of Taumarunui, the back way, the less traffic-congested way, so I had plenty of room to push my pram on the verge without worrying about passing cars and trucks. I had forty-two kilometers, a marathon to go, and Google Maps tells me I should have done it in nine hours. But I must confess to getting a ride up the largest, longest hill on the route when my vicar friends Val and Lance Riches came by in their van.

I was grateful for the ride to the top but could not suppress the nagging disquiet that I had not fulfilled what I set out to do. That nagging only strengthened my desire to do the whole distance, or whatever else I set out to do, with more integrity. On my second big walk, a year later down the South Island, I called on that desire for integrity and walked every inch of the 950 kilometers (about 600 miles). But this was the first when I was, if I'm honest, too lax with myself and my calling.

My boost up the big hill, and a mile or so farther on, got me to my destination, a farming family near Mapiu and the Mapiu school hall where I was to perform. It was a small audience but two were especially welcome. Keen to catch my performance but disappointed they'd missed it until now, they had driven for almost an hour east toward Taumarunui before turning north to catch up with me.

Twice before they had come to my rescue, and I was happy to be able to give them some spiritual food in return. The first rescue was after my work car skidded off the road and I ended in a ditch. My friend, a farmer, and a quiet gentle man, on a tractor nearby, pulled me out and was happy to do so. The second time, I had a similar mishap and needed his help again. I failed to take a sharp corner and my car left the road, thumped into a fence sideways, and became quite stuck. I walked to the nearest farmhouse for help and was surprised and a little chagrined to see him again. He just smiled and, with his tractor, extricated me without demur. Our next encounter, with St. Mark, was my chance to say thanks properly. But the final "thank you" goes to them and the long journey they made on the gospel's behalf. Country people are used to going long distances for social contact, and to pulling people out of the ditches around their property. I am glad to know them.

The next day was forty kilometers (twenty-five miles) to Te Kuiti, where my friend Mike Regan was editor of the local newspaper. I had counted on him for advance publicity. and now for accommodation. He even wrote a review of my performance, in the school hall, to about fifty people. He managed to leave out his agnostic skepticism, which is healthy, or unhealthy depending on how you look at it. And his wife Sheryl Mai, gave me a lift out of town to get my day going well. I had to do fifty kilometers (thirty miles) to Te Awamutu and I needed a considerable boost. She got me to Otorohanga which shaved seventeen kilometers (ten and a half miles) off the journey. This was the biggest cheating I had done so far or would ever do again. barring the injury that lay a few days in the future.

At Te Awamutu, the local Bible society hosted me in another school hall and a group from Cambridge made a twenty-five kilometer (fifteen mile) cross-country journey from the small private seminar I had contacted in one of my pre-publicity sorties. My familiar opening, declaring that this is the good news about Jesus Christ, the son of God, was getting more and more part of me. Twenty-five years later it still takes me by surprise and fills me with delight, which is what it's supposed to do, isn't it?

I stayed with my Aunt Grace in Hamilton, pushing my pram through central and suburban parts of that large city, and confessed, over dinner with her and my cousins, that I felt like the original bag lady going through the city streets in such a fashion. Another good crowd from the local branch of the Bible Society in New Zealand made me feel I was on the right track.

By this time, I had earned the interest and support of a local organizer, Mel Bowen from Rotorua who had arranged for me to stay with a pastor in the next town, Huntly. But first I had to walk to Ngaruawahia the back way, along the right bank of the Waikato River, and it was nearly dark when I got into Huntly and found my accommodation and place to perform.

In Huntly, I encountered the often-ignored problem of people reading while I am acting. It had always been a problem for me. For some reason, that I constantly struggled with, I resented people reading while I was acting. It was hard to stop feeling that they were checking up on me. I told myself that I had worked hard to memorize it and part of the delight of seeing solo theatre was the way it brought Jesus and Peter, Pontius Pilate, and many others, to life. Also, the readers were probably not using the same translation as the CEV and thus were constantly comparing what I said to the slight variations in whatever Bible their head was buried in.

As you watch a solo performance, characters appear in front of your eyes, the result of the actor and audience combining in a "willing suspension of disbelief", as Samuel Taylor Coleridge called it. It is a rewarding experience, diminished by reading it. When I see people reading, I smile inwardly and know that Jesus would prefer me to think, "Father forgive them, they know not what they do". I am sorry they are not getting as much out of it as I have put in, and once or twice I have, churlishly and quite rudely, asked them to stop.

So, in Huntly, a group of young people, came in late but I told myself that did not matter; I was delighted to see them, especially as they came and sat down the front. They picked up Bibles from the pews and started reading. I just carried on, presenting Mark to the group further back that did not have their heads bowed and therefore were communicating with me.

But when the front row started making comments to each other about a small mistake I'd made, because they had the version I was using, the CEV, I stopped and walked over to them. "Look, this is a test of memory and I feel you guys are not taking it the right way."

"Sorry," they said. "We were just amazed that you were so close, most of the time."

Of course, I was close, I try to be spot on. But there are often reasons people prefer to read than simply listen. English may not be their native language and they are more comfortable reading and hearing, as I have experienced. Or the habit of reading may be so ingrained that they automatically reach for the Bible when it is quoted. But recently, I spotted a woman in the congregation holding her Bible high, at eye level, as I read a lesson from the lectern. I smiled at that because that's how my mother held a book as she read to her three children. At that moment, all angst about audiences reading disappeared. My proud heart was softened by remembering a mother's love.

The next morning, in Huntly, I woke to a massive bruise that enveloped my right calf muscle. My exertions had produced broken blood vessels, and the injury was gross and alarming. An emergency doctor prescribed instant rest for a week. My host found me a ride to cover the one hundred kilometers (sixty miles) to Auckland, where I stayed with my brother for the duration of the same three days I'd have needed to cover the distance on foot. I solved the problem of how to walk across the busy Auckland Harbor Bridge (where no pedestrians were allowed) by taking the ferry, to Devonport, where I was expected for a performance and the next day caught the bus to a town further north. I had no more gigs planned, so I went looking for a backpackers' hostel. I found one on the outskirts of town. It was run by a smug, middle-aged woman who got more than she bargained for when she initially turned me away.

She took one look at the pram I'd pushed from Taumarunui, less the car and bus rides, and said she was not giving accommodation to Kiwi men, not then, not never. We New Zealand males have a reputation it seems, for many things and, in this case, for loitering around backpackers' hostels to steal food and making nuisances of ourselves with women guests. She said she'd had enough of that and only softened a little when I told her I was walking, when my leg recovered, to Cape Reinga performing Mark's gospel. She interrupted, "Well, we love the Lord," and put her nose in the air. She sniffed and said she kept a couple of good rooms for overseas tourists who might come by car. She sniffed again at my pram. "But not for Kiwis."

"However," she said, "you can have one since it's getting late now and nobody else will be coming." And, as we began to walk inside, she made the ultimate charitable observation, "You can't be too careful."

I stopped at the door. "Yes, you can. I have been walking the North Island telling the story of Jesus Christ who welcomed everybody and in His ministry, taught us to trust in faith, while He was on earth. He urged us to step out in faith, to accept everyone."

"We're in business and you can't be too careful," she said, as I left.

I walked up the hill to the camping ground and found a bare but warm cabin, for the next two nights, after which I planned to resume the walk. I told the man at the desk of my meeting with Mrs. Smug, and he said he knew her, a little personally but mainly by reputation.

"How did you get on with her? Didn't stay I see?" We both grinned.

Two days later, with my leg almost recovered, I resumed my walk, reaching the Bay of Islands in two more days and Kaitaia two days after that. I took the bus to Cape Reinga instead of walking for three more days and thus completed my first hikoi. Once back in Taumarunui, Mel Bowen from Rotorua and I began mounting a series of performances on behalf of the society, They took me, at weekends, all over his area of Waikato/Bay of Plenty, to Rotorua (twice) and Tauranga, Te Aroha, Taupo, where I met the chaplain of a prison farm. Each trip reaffirmed the good fortune I had to be based in the middle of everywhere, not the middle of nowhere at all.

The Taupo performance was a fundraiser to send Bibles to Iraq, at the height of the U.S./U.K. invasion and subsequent debacle in that country. We raised enough for 1,000 books in contrast with the instruments of destruction that war-torn country was getting at the time.

Each performance fed my nagging desire to do a little more, the desire and the unrest grew, and finally, after about ten performances for the society, I convinced myself that only a walk across America would satisfy that craving, and that I only had to interest leaders of even one denomination to make the journey plain sailing, though walking might be difficult. I put a lot of things before the cart, I realised as I looked back. The most burdensome was my rash conviction that the U.S. wanted me, maybe not yet, but that was just a matter of time, especially if I put myself in God's hands. I quit my job and sold my car. I stepped out in faith. I told myself I only had to contact church leaders and doors would open. It was not that simple, nothing like.

I was surprised calls were not returned and thus I could not tell anyone of my plan to finance my trip with performances along Route 66. I spent a week trying to contact church leaders and finally set off from Santa Monica pier, where I had never seen so many homeless people, and walked about thirty kilometers (twenty miles) a day for a week, with my pack on, until I reached San Bernadino.

After a while I thought pushing a shopping cart with the pack on board would be easier. I found an abandoned one quite quickly and set off. I had no idea that I was imitating the life and transport style that so many homeless people adopt. But I quickly realized the impression I was making when a young African-American man walked quickly toward me with a wide grin and shouted, "Hey, that's my mother's cart!", and walked away, laughing. I stayed in some rough motels to save money. One of them was proud to have been the filming location of *Attack of the 50-foot Woman,* released in 1958. But the churches I passed on the route, officially Route 66, intrigued me. It was quite a shock for an innocent Kiwi to find them locked.

After a week I reached San Bernadino and was about to head into the region of the Mojave Desert. With still no word from the church leaders I decided to quit and return to New Zealand. I am not going into specifics about whom I tried to contact. That was a long time ago and the obstacles then have been turned into opportunities now. The reward of perseverance has to begin with disappointment. Otherwise there is nothing to rise above.

It was, and still is, a twelve-hour flight and most people get some sleep over the quieter parts of the Pacific. But not me. Through the long flight, I analyzed what had gone wrong and decided I had relied too much on chance and optimism. I had not used faith to plan properly and to rely on sound assurance. I'd do better next time.

CHAPTER TWO

TOWARD THE END of the flight, I decided to walk the length of the South Island and I gave myself two months to plan. I would leave from Picton at the top of the island and walk to Bluff, at the bottom. It was now April and two months ahead lay the early winter month of June, and the cold, wet and miserable July. At this point I must acknowledge the strong and vital support of the Bible Society in New Zealand which asked at least two of their employees, the district organizers for the northern and southern regions of the society in the South Island, to find places along the route for me to perform, to find hospitality along the route too. As I write, I am filled with renewed gratitude for their Christianity-in-action deeds. Deeds that profited us both, because we split the collections.

I did a little organizing myself, phoning the few contacts I had, and one came up trumps. He was the chaplain of the Rangipo prison farm in the center of the North Island. I had met him when I performed Mark in Taupo, where he was a member of the society, even though it was a fifty kilometer (thirty mile) journey to attend. He invited me to stay with him and his family on my drive to Wellington for the start of the walk, turning the long one-day drive from Auckland to Wellington into two short ones. So, Rangipo was to be my first step on the journey south. I had often seen the turnoff from the main road, the sign pointing to the prison farm which was an almost tangible reminder not to try hitchhiking from there. That sign, "Rangipo Prison," would be a charming but unproductive backdrop for anyone putting their thumb up and asking for a ride further south. I'd hitched that road a lot in my college days, but I'd never stopped, or started, from there. And if I had, I'd have put distance between me and any sign that suggested I'd escaped recently. Not that they did, as my host assured me. It was very low security. Nevertheless, I didn't know where to look when I started to perform. In front of me were just seven prison inmates, my audience and forget jokes about a captive audience. These guys came and went with more freedom than any of the fifty or so groups who had seen my solo theatre version of Mark's gospel. These mobile seven compared interestingly with the stationary 1,500 or so of previous performances. These lads would slope off throughout the evening when they'd had enough, and drift into the room when they wanted more. So, the average size of the audience was seven.

That's some average for a prison farm with winter nights closing. And if they were daunted by me, though they gave no indication they were, I was a little dismayed at the size of the audience that my message was attracting and I let a little prayer creep in that I might meet larger numbers in the South Island.

Usually, in the performance, I would rest my eyes on various audience members as I worked through the text, making sure to include as many as possible as often as I could. But this night I didn't know where to look when in Chapter Two, and with their attention spans not too stretched, I came to Jesus explaining to his audience, probably more than seven, that He didn't come to ask *good* people to be His followers. He said, "I came to invite …": I didn't know where to look. I settled for just over their heads as I released the word, after a suitable pause, "Sinners."

So, the reaction I got was just aural. I didn't see their delighted expressions, their sudden realization that our Lord's message was for them too. I just heard a communal exhalation and the word, the release of, "Yes" on collective lips. "Yes," I thought. The prisoners were all from the sexual offenders' unit and were separated from the rest of the community. This I knew. I guess they knew I knew, though that mattered not.

It certainly gave me a fresh insight and perspective as I worked through such stories as Jesus telling his disciples that someone who causes even the least of his followers to sin would be better off thrown into the ocean with a heavy weight tied around their neck. I wondered if any of those in front of me had done that. And immediately I asked myself why I did not apply the same judgment to regular congregations and audiences. Who was I to assume I was telling Jesus's story to those already familiar with it? And why should I not ask myself why *every* member of the audience, in a cathedral or prison workroom, wherever it was, was with me in this great adventure, the telling of God's good news?

In that prison one young man sat transfixed. His gaze never left my face and later I asked the chaplain what he was inside for.

"Preventive detention."

"You mean they have thrown away the key? Why?"

"Third rape."

This sexual offender would never see the outside world. He was institutionalized and was making the prison farm his home. Because of that, or maybe because of his calm acceptance, he carried a certain leadership quality and showed others the way. Like his urgent attention, his absolute concentration showed the others how to behave. I took that tale, of the sharp "yes!" from my "sinners", with me down the South Island – and as a result, more than one leader of a congregation was waiting to hear it from his flocks' lips when I came to the second chapter of Mark's gospel.

Day One–Wellington to Picton (by ferry)

Two days later I set off from Wellington by the Cook Strait Ferry, and contemplated what lay ahead. But not for long, as I quickly realized I had no idea what was in store for me. I knew 966 kilometers (600 miles) over thirty-five days must be covered, but nothing more. Still waiting in the wings were the highs and lows, the welcome few who came through snowbound streets in Rangiora; the South Korean girl who had never heard the gospel before, the packed hall in Milton; the twin nine-year-old boys who met me in Clinton and sent me on my way to Gore, along the main highway, nicknamed "Presidential Highway" for good reason.

That first morning, I watched as I wondered, and Wellington Harbor put on a display. In such perfect, still weather it ranks among the most beautiful of the world's capital city settings. Winter had officially begun on June 1, but this day, June 7, 2002, was like a still autumn day.

I was on the mid–morning sailing. The sparkling clean air had traces of the morning's near-frost, and in the blue above there was nothing but the earlier movements of airplanes' vapor trails and the sun, skirting the hills that surrounded the harbor. The blue below was still enough to record the movement of ships long after they'd glided out to sea and the patterns of tidal movement.

The hills are sprinkled with hundreds and thousands of tenacious houses where unsmiling Victorian men had made their homes since the 1840s. But it was God that smiled when he made Wellington Harbor and it was the warmth of the blessing from the Bible society president and senior staff that sent me on my way rejoicing, by this three-hour ferry crossing, out of the harbor and across Cook Strait, on a perfect day to start a journey, though I honestly did not expect St. Mark to be in demand when the ferry sailed into Picton.

The remarkable thing about the walk was the recollection it gave me of every other time I had travelled that road, by car mostly but also by bus, and often by "auto-stop", the charming French phrase for hitchhiking, in my college student days. I was seven for my first arrival in Picton. It was about the same time of year, winter, but in the middle of a storm on a less-seaworthy tub, and before the days of roll-on/roll-off ferries. It was 1955, and our family was moving to the South Island. I remember I was too young to read "joined-up" writing and also the only one of our family of five not seasick on the short crossing.

What a contrast this gloriously still and warm (in the sun) day made. I met the expected *Picton Herald* reporter/photographer, and we walked back to the end of the pier for a photograph and short interview. It was my first interview and the first time I heard a question I was to get often, "Why?"

Oh, I was to have fun with that question in the next month. Being one, I knew you must think on your feet with journalists and assess how they will process what you tell them, before deciding what and how to tell them. They don't want to hear, "I don't know," because it's a rare journalist that will not exploit that indecision and create a great opening paragraph, such as, "*Geoffrey Darling is walking the South Island performing Mark's gospel and he has no clue why.*" They want a jam and bread story about a guy, setting off, 966 kilometers to go. They've done it before with other adventurers, charity cyclists, stilt walkers of the world, etc. They all leave from Picton and all credit to the paper for telling their stories.

The paper of June 8, 2002, did not have a large, resonant biblical quote, or say that I was called to do this, or that I felt a certainty and completeness the more I planned this walk, which at this stage was still a consolation prize for the failure of not getting far on Route 66 in the U.S.A.

Frankly, I have no idea what it said. I was a few days' south before it came out and when I went looking for it, 20 years later, I learned the paper had closed. There's a lesson there somewhere, But I do know I kept it secular and so set a pattern that was repeated with newspaper interviews in Ashburton, Timaru, and Invercargill as well as a television appearance in Dunedin. I never had any difficulty getting the media interested. This story was good harmless stuff for them and a welcome change from the mayhem they might be called on to report without warning.

On reflection, it asks an interesting question along the lines of, "What is the point of doing something like this, walking from town to town and performing Mark's gospel, re-enacting the arrival of Jesus and His disciples in a town and bringing the people out to hear the good news, without proclaiming it from the rooftops, in every available newspaper outlet?" A debate for another time.

I had not planned a performance in Picton, as far as I could recall. I intended to check in with the Picton Anglican Church, which I did after I found a place in the dormitory of a local backpackers' hostel. I quickly checked out again when the vicar and his wife invited me to stay with them. They told me one of the parishioners had been asking all day, "Has St Peter arrived yet?" So "St Peter" went to stay at the vicarage and met a welcoming congregation.

It was a graceful stone church, built by the parishioners' hard work of hauling the stones from a remote location several hours' drive away. It sat on the edge of a small village-green-type roundabout, doubtless viewed by many speeding from the ferry to begin their adventure on the "mainland". For the first of my performances in the South Island, that evening I performed in bare feet, as usual.

I love acting bare-footed. I always have. It feels as though one's movement and posture are given an earthy directness by contact with the floor. Ever since I first performed *The Rime of the Ancient Mariner* solo in 1986, I have been exploring the genre of solo theatre. I could not have done St. Mark's gospel without conquering the simpler and shorter ballad by Coleridge (forty minutes), which I have presented more than one hundred times. I could still, at the drop of a hat, so snugly are the lines embedded in the place that lines go to rest in, which will always be a mystery to me. I poured more lines into my brain with a look at my Alzheimer's afflicted mother's life in 1998, an analysis of Shakespeare and the supernatural in 1999, which brought Rev. Dr. Jim Stuart's invitation to perform Mark's gospel the next year. But this is starting to sound like a CV.

The Picton church's floor was a little chilly but those gathered, about thirty, were generous and warm and to this day remember the time that St Peter walked in. On looking back on the walk and the eighteen performances of Mark that the walk produced, I turned my thoughts to Jesus's walks and boat rides across Lake Galilee. The discussions he led while walking, and the crowds that followed those walks, were always on my mind as I prepared and undertook the many walks of my own. This account of the South Island journey, and what went before and after, would not be complete without also discussing Jesus's many journeys and marking each performance with thoughts on one of Jesus's journeys. After Picton, the first performance, I thought about Jesus's many journeys and forms of journeys.

> "Now as he walked by the sea of Galilee, he saw Simon and Andrew his brother casting a net into the sea; for they were fishers. And Jesus said unto them. Come ye after me, and I will make you to become fishers of men." Mark 1:16-17 (KJV)

> In the modern version which I used in performances, this passage has Jesus saying he would show them how to bring in people instead of fish. But a quick dip into the internet site "BibleGateway" shows that

even quite modern versions favor the phrase "fishers of men", not just the KJV. Such a short phrase, so apt and easily understood, conveys much. Other variations, found randomly, include: "I will send you out to fish for people", "I will make you fish for men", and "I'll send you to catch people *instead of fish*." None are contradictory and all support the original writer, St. Mark But none are as pithily poetical as "fishers of men." In Mark 1, Jesus begins his preaching before gathering even His first disciples, and the preaching was itinerant, as it remained for the best part of his time in the Holy Land. The Bible commentator B. Harvie Branscomb, writing in *The Gospel of Mark,* part of the *Moffat New Testament Commentary*, says the practice of religious leaders traveling with their disciples was common at the time of Jesus. Branscomb suggests that the phrase "Come ye after me" meant "Be my disciple." But while other religious teachers were teaching their disciples established works, for example, The Talmud and the Torah, Jesus had his eyes on the souls of people and made sure His disciples knew that. From this passage, Jesus appears to be picking four fishermen at random, but a look at John 1 shows that Andrew and Simon Peter had earlier heard John the Baptist proclaiming Jesus as the Messiah and that they had met Jesus.

Day Two–Picton to Blenheim (twenty-eight kilometers or eighteen miles)

An early night followed, and it was still dark at 6.30 a.m. when I climbed the hill, known as Elevation, bound for Blenheim. Naturally, and, let's face it, by the Grace of God, the vicarage had provided a hearty breakfast and there was just a hint of frost, for the second day in a row. It was still dark enough to let Picton's lights twinkle a farewell, as I climbed the narrow streets and walked out into the country. Blenheim was at least six hours' walk away. I knew that. I'd done it before, on January 2, 1968, to be exact. That was the Marlborough Walk, an enactment, since discontinued, of the pioneers who landed from ships in Picton, at the head of the beautiful Marlborough Sounds and walked to the more useful, flat, and productive Wairau Plains back in the 1840s, to found the town of Blenheim (named after Blenheim Palace, the home of the Duke of Marlborough, in an age when Britain was regarded as the "mother country" by most settlers).

In 1968, I walked it with some college friends. The locals did not have the walk on January 1, because too many would have too many sore heads. Since January 2 is also a holiday in New Zealand (a Scottish tradition), it seemed a good time to have it then. I know it took me six hours, but I did not have a pack on my back or an extra thirty-four years on my heels.

A purple mail truck and trailer unit was among the large vehicles that passed me that morning. We, the driver and me, did not know it then but every day, a little later each day and a little farther down the road, that purple truck would pass me, wondering, "Who is this guy?" as I would, and their big toot would be followed by my big wave. On the second day it was two toots, the next day three, and so on. We enjoyed the game but that was all we knew about each other, for five or six days. The sun and the temperature rose, and the miles melted.

After the initial incline to Elevation, the road turned flat. It followed a gentle valley that was partly adorned with unproductive scrub and was partly grazing land. A river and its flat, a swamp and its willows, it was a welcoming introduction to the South Island.

Morning tea came at a handy petrol station and lunch at a wayside hotel. I was going to make Blenheim in about seven hours, including a stop for tea and lunch. This was not bad going, and the journey and the fitness could only get better. There was little traffic except when a car ferry docked at Picton, about every three hours. For about half an hour after arriving, they sped in convoy to Blenheim and points south.

I'd been part of the phenomenon from time to time—once in the wee small hours of a summer midnight crossing when the convoy stayed connected for about eighty miles. And now I would see it repeated for several days until I got far enough south for the convoys to have dispersed themselves to nothing. But that large purple truck kept on coming, day after day.

In sight of the small town of Blenheim, a young man stopped. He was the first of many to stop opposite me, I walked facing the oncoming traffic, and one of the most interesting. He asked if I was the guy performing Mark that night and I crossed over the road to tell him, "Yes, sure."

He asked me if I'd read the St. James' gospel and showed me a copy in his glove box. I admitted my ignorance and invited him to my presentation, at the Salvation Army Citadel, that evening. He said he knew the captain, with whom I was staying, and would try to make it.

I walked on into Blenheim: The census in 2001 put Blenheim's population at 26,550, a change of 3.3 percent since 1996, the same as New Zealand's. It is the capital of the Marlborough province, which can lay claim to starting the modern wine industry in New Zealand. In the late 1970s, the giant wine-making company, Montana, produced Sauvignon Blanc, among other varieties, which led to confidence that New Zealand could produce exciting wine. I was to see a lot more of those grapes on the fertile Wairau Plains as I walked on. A lot, lot more.

The walk presented little difficulty, apart from the several bridges I needed to cross on the main road, State Highway 1. The smaller ones were no real problem, but the bigger ones were very difficult, offering little room to walk. So, I used the lulls in traffic, which eventually appeared, to dash for the safety of the other side. It was difficult with a pack on and these bridges presented a problem I never really solved. I just found temporary solutions.

It was now mid-afternoon and time to meet my host. I was delighted to learn that Jim Wescomb, the Bible society representative for the top half of the South Island, was going to be there too. It was a modest house. Lacking a spare room, some younger members of the family were delegated to sleep on couches in the living room, while Jim and I took the twin beds in their room. Bless them.

But it was a house of great warmth, as well. About 4 p.m. and less than an hour before the winter sun set in the west, the fire in the firebox was pumping heat. This was happening in every South Island home at this stage of the winter; and would continue until August. It was a lively performance, a delighted small audience sat attentively, my "St. James gospel" friend appeared but did not stay long, and a few decided to follow my story in a Bible sitting in a pew in front of them. After the Blenheim presentation, the second on the journey, I looked to:

"And in the morning, rising up a great while before day, He went out, and departed into a solitary place, and there prayed." Mark 1:35 (KJV)

It occurred to me, as I walked along in quiet contemplation of such things, that Jesus often sought solitude to pray. This was part of His journey to find quiet places for prayer and, consistent with his words in the Sermon on the Mount (Matthew 6), that prayer should be in private, not long-winded and repetitious. Our Father, as the sermon says, knows what we need before we ask Him. In other parts of Mark's gospel, Jesus sends his disciples away, even to the other side of Lake Galilee, so He can be alone and pray. And there is the prayer in the Garden of Gethsemane, also in private, and with sleeping disciples nearby. This time Jesus's prayer is in preparation for His ministry in Galilee. He returns from prayer with His Father to announce the next step, to go to nearby towns of Galilee to tell of the good news, and adds that this is why He had come. Branscomb claims that Mark believes Jesus knew He was the Messiah only from the moment of Baptism, though the Bible commentator admits it is a moot point, and certainly not supported by the other gospels. For example, Luke 2 tells of the twelve-year-old Jesus going about His Father's business in Jerusalem.

Day Three—Blenheim to Seddon (twenty-three kilometers or fourteen miles)

Seddon is a small town in Marlborough, south of Blenheim, and named for former Prime Minister Richard John Seddon (1845-1906). It's close to the mouths of the Awatere and Blind rivers, and is also close to the Lake Grassmere salt works, a major local industry. The town's best-known structure is a joint single-lane road-rail bridge spanning the Awatere River, which was due to be replaced by two separate structures.

Well, that told me what I wanted to know. With just twenty-three kilometers ahead and Jim to carry my pack, it would be quite a simple day. Being winter, it dawned late and overcast but I was early on the road before my host of the Salvation Army had risen, before Jim, and before, as it turned out, McDonald's, which I was counting on for breakfast. Not opening until 8 a.m., it forced me to wait in the growing mist and the threatening cold. Still, I was comfortably clad.

It was a reminiscing and nostalgic look at Blenheim—two years of my childhood, from seven to nine, had been spent there and of course, it had changed; though not much, not enough to allay fear for its future. However, with wine as the constant in a constantly increasing number of New Zealand lives, there was a feeling of small satisfaction about the place. i.e., it was small but satisfied.

Soon after leaving, and with no ill effects from the eighteen miles the day before, I found an old cobb cottage, made from planks and plaster between the planks, still being restored. It was as if Blenheim was in less of a hurry to recover its pioneer past than the rest of New Zealand. One day it would be worth a visit but not yet.

A few kilometers down the road, a huge winery, that made a statement about the new wealth of the previously struggling region, reared up, three stories high and the same appearance as a modern dairy factory. Leisure and tourism went hand in hand. Wine and food festivals and the scenic beauty of the region attracted people from all over the world and contrasted dramatically with the early efforts of the pioneers, who were too busy grasping a living from the soil and from the sheep's backs to create much wealth.

It struck me, as I walked up the first hills of the day, that a country that has leisure has an abundance of wealth. True wealth lies not in the raw materials needed for industrial production but in the time to savor one's existence. The Bible talks about that, and I kept on climbing.

The plains quickly spread below. A steady stream of cars was not too concerned at my presence around blind corners, but I was concerned about the absence of any roadside stopping place. The road was all barren, challenging hills between me and Seddon which was, at my current pace, still five hours away.

A fast walking pace is four miles her hour but I was doing three. I worked in kilometers, having become accustomed to them when New Zealand converted about thirty years before. Knowing both systems, I am sort of "ambidextrous". I tried to march at six kph, or one kilometer every ten minutes, and was delighted whenever the kilometer marker post would come up inside that time. That was on good days when my pack was carried. As one kilometer equals 5/8 of a mile, six kph equals 3.75 mph, but I was on the flat, and Jim was taking my pack to Seddon, the first but not the last time the pack got a ride. If I added them up, I would say the pack was carried about half the way. Jesus found kind people, sometimes strangers to carry the pack. For example, on this second day, Jim took the pack to my hosts in Seddon before driving south where I would see him about ten days later. The next day the pastor at the tiny hamlet, Martin Harrison, arranged for the pack to go via the daily laundry van to my next stopping place, where the road again met the Pacific Ocean, at Kekerengu.

Once, an old couple, and now I am getting two weeks ahead of myself, stopped and asked if I wanted a lift. Let's remember that though I followed the main road, State Highway 1, it was never more than a dual carriageway and I could talk easily with drivers across the road, going in the same direction (because I always walked facing the on-coming traffic). I thanked them and suggested they might like to give the pack a lift. Scary? Not really. If they were open enough to offer a lift, they would not run off with my pack. I knew my compatriots, the good and the bad.

But that was my pack's adventure. Back to mine. On top of the first saddle out of the plains that Blenheim sat so well on and along the plateau that led to Seddon. Jim passed me at about 2 p.m. and was surprised to find me so far down the track. I could see Seddon resting in a small valley below and the foothills of the Southern Alps, the backbone of the South Island, appeared to the west. It was still grey and overcast but the road was interesting and only one obstacle lay between me and a couple of hours rest before the evening performance.

This is quite a famous bridge, about 150 meters (500 ft.) across the Awatere River; a single lane controlled by lights and built for much less powerful machines than the juggernauts that passed me at regular intervals. It was Sunday and I soon learned that no trains traveled on the South Island main trunk railway on Sundays. I stored that information for future use.

Rather than dodge the cars, trucks, semi-trailers, etc., I scrambled up the bank and crossed above the road. Trucks rumbled below me, *just* below me, and the river swished just below that. The taller trucks made it quite fun as I stuck to the walkway beside the rails. They seemed just inches away from me. It was my first encounter with the vagaries of the bridge system in the South Island, and it was tremendous fun.

In Seddon, I asked at the local corner store for directions to my host and, as I expected, the teenage girls all knew him. They were interesting, to talk to, obviously wishing there was more to life than getting a milkshake at the corner store on a Sunday afternoon and imagining that the bright lights of the big city would make it all better. They knew Pastor Martin, who wore many hats, as it turned out. He was a Presbyterian minister, husband of the local doctor and father of four boys, a fire-fighter with tales of drought-inspired pasture fires that two years ago threatened the town.

Just a short distance under my belt but I was nevertheless tired and asked for a brief nap before the evening performance at Martin's church. It was a delightful little church. Martin's family crowded into the front pew and that was great. So often, almost always in fact, people love to sit at the back and with the advent of radio mikes and sound systems, they feel justified in doing so. Like every actor, I find it less encouraging when they choose to do so, because a gap needs to be crossed, with effort (invariably mine).

I have a big voice and can use it, so electronic enhancement is an obstruction. There is often a sound person at the back changing the volume, and this was the case in a couple of places further south where I was persuaded to use a microphone.

But in this tiny church, with a long and inspiring history, I had no doubt, the acoustics were clear. Martin's sons were valuable props at one stage, when Jesus called his twelve apostles to him. At this stage, I'd go around the audience and often single out my hosts for the evening as *"Peter",* etc. Then I'd take their eyes and name them one of the other disciples, *"James and John, Andrew, Phillip, Bartholomew, Matthew, Thomas"* (actors used little mnemonics, in mine was All Points Bulletin & MT) that's eight. *"James son of Alphaeus and Thaddeus"* (easy to remember because of the two ... eus words. Then to finish. *"The others were Simon known as the Eager One and Judas Iscariot who later betrayed Jesus."*

It was a very happy Sunday evening, dark when we finished, and I met several people who were very interested in my mission. Two invited me to lunch at their motel in Ward the next day, about twenty-three kilometers (fifteen miles) before lunch. I decided I could do that, but I needed an early start, five hours at 5 kph, certainly doable, and then another twenty kilometers after lunch. A piece of cake if I did not eat too much of it. My journey was done for the day, but Jesus's journey, that I thought on as I went to sleep, had just begun.

> "But he went out, and began to publish it much, and to blaze abroad the matter, insomuch that Jesus could no more openly enter into the city, but was without in desert places: and they came to him from every quarter.: Mark 1:45 (KJV)

> Here we have Jesus unable to travel openly because of the public awareness of His healing powers, notably of healing a person with leprosy who talked to many people despite Jesus's warning not to. This is the start of another journey for Jesus; i.e. His tightrope walk between openly healing people and wanting to keep that healing secret. For example, when He brings Jairus' daughter back from assumed death, and when He heals a man who is deaf and nonspeaking, He asks the onlookers to say nothing about it. He asks a blind man whose sight He restores, not to go back to his

village. In Mark 7, Jesus stays in someone's house near Tyre. He does not want people to know He is there, but they find out anyway.

After the Transfiguration in Mark 8, He asks Peter, James, and John, witnesses to seeing Him talking to Moses and Elijah, not to say anything about what they had seen. When Peter says "Thou art the Christ", after Jesus asks, "Whom say ye that I am?", (KJV) Jesus goes on to ask the disciples not to repeat that assertion.

Day Four–Seddon to Kekerengu (forty-three kilometers or twenty-seven miles)

I set off in the early morning, in the traditionally dry winter of the province, sheltered by the western hills that were growing rapidly, despite my walking pace, into strong mountains known as the Seaward Kaikouras. The road was windy and the blessing of the family was warming, the forecast was fine, and lunch awaited at noon at the Tui Motel, Ward.

The road led past Lake Grassmere where salt is manufactured, and I was surprised to find little reference to it on the internet. Then I realized I was using the wrong spelling. I was looking for Grasmere like the lake in the English Lake District, the haunt of Wordsworth and Coleridge, and not Grassmere. I found an entry on the internet about Grassmere. It explained that seawater was pumped into the 688-hectare (1700-acre) main lake continuously, throughout summer. Then, as evaporation strengthened the sea water, it was pumped into a series of ponds, where further evaporation took place. The saturated brine then went into crystallization ponds for the hot summer months.

Once crystallized, the salt crust was lifted from the bottom of the ponds and taken to one of the two washing plants, where it is washed in brine and then stacked in piles twenty meters (one chain) high. The snowy stacks of salt were something of a landmark, readily visible by day and night from the Blenheim - Christchurch highway. The low rainfall was also ideal for salt production.

Reading that, I understood for the first time what Jesus meant in

Mark's gospel when he urged the disciples to have salt among themselves and live at peace with each other.

I had always known about Lake Grassmere and would like to say that this was the first time I'd stood beside it, as opposed to driving or riding in a train or bus past. But as I walked past it brought back the memory of a wild episode in my young life; aged eighteen and on an impulse, inspired by the tranquility of Wellington Harbor, I decided to go to Christchurch. I took the ferry to Blenheim and a classmate, who I barely knew except that he was a Christian, invited me into his home for the night.

The next day I bussed to Christchurch and went into a quiz show, won my way on stage, and into the final that was to be held the next weekend. The prize was a trip for two to Australia and worth showing up for again. But, being a student, funds for a second trip in a week were limited, so I hitchhiked. On that second journey, darkness fell and passing cars stopped passing. This was 1967 and a different era, where trust among the young without cars was matched by compassion among those young, and not-so-young, *with* cars. It was a frequent option for me and remained so for many years. But this night, Lake Grassmere, or rather the long grass beside the road, was my bed as I lay down and tried to sleep. I shivered and struggled to rest on the cold ground and promised myself I would never do this again. Unfortunately, I did but that's another story.

As I walked, I realized that this journey was going to remind me at some stage, and in some way, of every trip I had made on this road. But I had much distance still to go before that noon lunch date. By now, the third day on the road, I had figured out how to tell how fast I was going. A little-known fact, and something motorists neither notice nor need to notice, is the placement of kilometer markers on the side of the road. What look like ordinary markers, spaced fifty to one hundred meters apart with luminous strips for night driving, have a new number marking every kilometer. Once I worked that out, I would look for them about every ten minutes, since I was walking at 6 kph (about 3.5 mph). Alternatively, I used farmers' gate numbers which were numbered from the nearest main road in tenths of a kilometer. Number 658 meant 6.58 kilometers from the main road, and 688 meant

6.88 km or another 300 meters down the road, then 718 means 7.18 kilometers. Is that understood? Don't worry, you do not have hugely long and mostly empty roads with little else to think about.

Ward, which I reached in good time, was where my grandfather was principal of a two-teacher school. I looked for the school because I'd heard the family legend, that in the late 1930s, the school burned down and the volunteer firefighters called into the schoolhouse on the way to the fire, to tell Grandpa it was burning down. I heard it as a child and, naturally, it was told light-heartedly, rather than alarm me, so it did not stick as a horror story. It wasn't. I found Ward probably no bigger than at the time of the fire, when my grandparents, my mother, and her brother and sister, spent his last teaching years.

The school was still there, and the motel. It's a popular spot for travelers who like to drive a little way south from the ferry before resting. While it was two and half days walk for me, it was just forty-five minutes for cars, buses, trucks, etc. Tending such a motel was an ideal life for a semi-retired couple and the pair welcomed me with great warmth, sharing their blessings in the form of a simple but love-given meal.

After an hour, at 1 p.m. with dark just four hours away and another twenty-three kilometers (fifteen miles) to go, I set off again. A road crew was relaxing after a good job done, the reconstruction of about two miles of highway. Relaxing? They sure were. Ahead were three kilometers (two miles) of the witches' hats to be picked up and only one (female) member of the crew was doing it. She was walking towards me, while four men lounged on the back of the truck. I made a joke to encourage her, as I passed them, and carried on.

Soon a car stopped. A man and a woman I recognized from the night before. She was the Reverend Miriam Taylor and Malcolm, her husband, was going to walk with me. He'd done it before when he accompanied a girl from my hometown, Rotorua, who had walked the length of New Zealand to raise money for charity. Girl from my home town did I say? Goodness, she was a Dame of the Realm. She had told him, and he told me in turn, that her loneliest moments on the walk were along the coast where I was headed. So, he decided to go with me for at least part of it.

Being Kiwis, we played the "Do You Know" game. No other country in the world can play it as well as we. With a population of just four million and many of those constantly moving, we usually know people in common, especially if we have a common interest, like Christianity.

We'd simply ask people's origins and if they knew someone we knew from there. I've been "playing" it all my life, without realizing it, and it's made for interesting conversations. New Zealanders have just one degree of separation between them. For example, when the Air New Zealand Erebus Disaster of November 1979 killed 257 passengers and crew on an Antarctic mountain, people either knew someone aboard or knew someone who knew someone. That's how close we are as a nation.

In this case, we discovered Keith and Jean Ross, my friends through the Anglican Church in Taumarunui. Malcolm Taylor was eager to get in touch. I had his number on my cell phone, called him and Malcolm and then me, chatted for a few minutes. Keith, whom I've mentioned twice in the early pages of this book, was very happy to hear my progress. Then Malcolm and I walked on to the coast where his ride was waiting and we parted, never to meet again. Well, we can't look into the future, but I am sure he looks back on that afternoon with fondness and delight, as do I. Being New Zealanders, we never say farewell forever. It was late afternoon and many more miles to go before my rest, but I found time to pause at St Oswald's on the coast.

Again, it's one of those places I'd passed and not stopped, too many times. This time I went inside and was particularly impressed by the majestic stained-glass window dedicated to St. Mark. We paused and the window and I communed together. Time was getting on and although I was expecting to meet my pack, that the Rev. Martin had sent on via the laundry truck, at Kekerengu, it was going to be touch and go whether I met it and my hosts before darkness fell at 5 p.m.

By now the huge pounding breakers of the South Pacific/Southern Ocean and the warm northwest wind were coming across the mountains reaching down towards the sea. A huge arch of cloud formed. It had dropped all its rain on the west coast of the South Island and, as snow, on the Southern Alps, and now on the east coast, it was dark, high, and dry. As the sun set, it sent a more magnificent sight than I have ever walked under.

The huge dark cloud lit up like a torch, changing as slowly as I was walking it seemed, and gave me an insight into that imponderable question, how many more sunsets will each of us see? For myself, I think I will be lucky to see another 2,000 but none of this magnitude, like a cape of many reds hanging from the dark, dry clouds, the eastern horizon playing its part with a separate glow, and the sea constantly swirling, eddying back and depositing again, colors in ways we have all seen a thousand times. From dark green at the start of the sunset to an increasinly ominous black. All this can be seen at 4.30 to 5 p.m. any winter's evening, available not on demand but set apart from the demands of modern life. I was still about three kilometers from my destination, as I watched the sky darken and wondered if I would be overtaken by the early nightfall. I had a reflector belt of my father's and there was little traffic on the road, but on the negative side, there were few safe places to walk. On my right, the side of the road I needed to walk to face the traffic, cliffs came right down to the roadside. I chose the left in the growing darkness and missed seeing a light truck that was coming, looking for me on the right side (his left). He'd been waiting at the petrol station/roadside restaurant stop, but as the darkness came quicker than any of us expected, he'd come north, looking for me.

The truck stopped down the road, turned, and came towards me, picking me up still a mile away from my destination. As I got into the welcome ride, I resolved to take no shortcuts and the next morning I asked to be dropped off where I'd been picked up, not at the wayside stop where I was headed. That practice I repeated several times on the journey. It was just a question of being true to myself so that in future years I could honestly say, on looking at a map of the South Island of New Zealand, "I walked that bit, all of it."

My host chatted on the way into the hills above Kekerengu. He'd blown up his farm bike the day before. When most people say that they mean, "scuttled the engine", or disabled it in some way. But this man had blown it up. It had caught on fire as he leaped for his life. But he was relaxed about it, even laughing as he told me.

His wife greeted me with the best welcome I could imagine. "Ah, you are walking for Jesus!" There was no performance that evening, but I put on my costume and presented a couple of chapters, singing for my supper as it were, before she did an hour's charity work for the Christian Radio Station, Radio Rhema. Between 9 and 10 p.m. once a week, she went on air and offered advice to troubled listeners. They were a middle-aged couple, with children grown and gone and they made me very welcome for no other reason than I was walking for Jesus. The next morning, the day dawned as brightly as the red sky last night had promised. I never could work out whether a red sky at night was a sailor's delight or a shepherd's, or who took warning when the sky was red in the morning.

Day Five–Kekerengu to Okiwi Bay (thirty kilometers or nineteen miles)

Dawn was late that midwinter morning and I remembered that I needed to go a mile or so up the road before walking back down. My hosts understood and were happy to oblige. They even gave me a packed lunch because they knew, and I was to find out, there would be nothing further down the road. So, the morning unfolded. I quickly made up the distance I had lost and round a bend in the road could see what lay before me, at least until lunchtime.

Large hills sloped down to within a mile or so of the road on my right and on the left, dunes, with the sea even farther left. It was an interesting coast, some parts black sand and in some parts black pebbles. I was heading for a camping ground at Okiwi Bay. about halfway to Kaikoura where another performance and another hospitable Christian house awaited.

It was more like early autumn than the start of winter on June 10, and I basked in the easy walking conditions. I was carrying my pack again for the first time in three days and I felt that weight. There was not much traffic. A car or truck would pass about every five minutes, so I did not have to get off the road much, not on fine days like today. The red sky of the night before had given way to a clear, perfect, 12C (54F) day. It was ideal for walking, and I slipped into a familiar routine of watching for the next marker post and revising a few passages of Mark's gospel that were getting a bit rusty.

When I began presenting the gospel, I left out Chapter 13, in which Jesus talks about the last days. But many people asked me why and I floundered for an explanation. If I were to do Mark's gospel, I was hardly qualified to make a judgment about what should and should not be left in. So, I learned it, on the road. It didn't take long. A few minutes revising a day and it quickly sank in.

I struggle to believe that Jesus's physical presence on earth is going to make this earth any better than His spiritual presence does right now if we let it. He said, "I am with you always" and He also said, "Be Ready." No more and no less.

Some years later I had a wonderful insight into this truth. It came from a wonderful production of Sir Peter Shaffer's masterpiece *Equus* in Cleveland, Ohio. The director poured all his great love for the play and his huge talent into a very successful production that had critics and the public alike raving and awestruck. He left after the first night saying he would try to come back, from Philadelphia, before the run ended. He did not but every performance was as acute and accurate to his guidance as we could make it and we always acted as if he was there, could be there, could be coming.

With the love we had for the man and his talent, we brought his creation to life every night of the month-long run. I have told the story to my brother-in-law Jeff, a pastor in a small mid-West church and he said he could see a sermon in that message.

I believe that Jesus rose from the dead and that he died for our sins and through the believing of that, and baptism, we are saved, and through the Grace of God. We are saved through his loving sacrifice, the miracle by which God became man turned full circle and Jesus the man became God. He warned us to be on our guard, and so we should be, and treat God's creation with the same love that He poured into it.

All I know is that in my experience of walking for a month on the incredibly beautiful South Island of New Zealand, I felt as though I was walking part of heaven. I learned Chapter 13 and easily found time to present it, like, Jesus delivering a lecture. It was like when Jesus called his followers together and told them if they wanted to follow Him they must take up their cross.

In that late autumn sun, I basked, even slept for half an hour at lunch, stretched out under poplar trees with the sun beating down in the last benevolent act of the dying summer, but I was spurred into action by the knowledge that four hours of daylight remained, as bright a day as it was.

After presenting me with large cliffs in the distance and telling me there lay my path, the road climbed steeply enough to force me to rest before leaving the sea and crossing the mighty Clarence River. And it was a crossing that needed some care. There was no real walkway, and I had a pack on my back. I had to pick my moments to stand on the roadway. Little was I to know it would be no easier the farther south I went.

Time was marching though I was not, and I forced myself to hurry; the darkness and a roadside camping ground arrived almost together at Okiwi Bay Beach. There were cabins, "Wonderful"; there was food available, "Even better." The accommodation offered that night was an old house bus that was not likely to go very far. It was mounted on blocks. There was not much of a selection at the office either. A can of baked beans and sausages was a banquet though, and a small radio was my entertainment. The news was that Prime Minister Helen Clark was calling for an early election, her excuse being she thought the time was right. Curious that she waited so long to announce an election the next time around, although the time was right then too.

Day Six–Okiwi Bay to Kaikoura (thirty kilometers or nineteen miles)

I was up before dawn the next morning, calculating the distance I had to walk before Kaikoura that afternoon. I snacked a breakfast and set off, after a shower at the common ablution block, such an icon of the New Zealand camping ground. Nobody else was about. A few caravans were staying a while, perhaps the whole winter. I had no idea. This was an idyllic spot, with the still sea sending a calming influence over the land in the early morning.

Round the first bend in the dark road, I could see the lights of my destination. Soon I stepped off the road that ran alongside the rocky coast to answer nature's call and went towards the sea itself. I think I felt its panic before I saw it; the cute baby seal staring up at me. Its mother was gone; she'd dived into the sea without a warning call to her offspring, as I approached. Then I saw not one but at least four in the grey dawn. So close, we were staring at each other. Did the little guys know I was as fascinated as they and about as harmless? This coast was populated by the whalers and sealers of the late 1700s and, before them, Māori had plundered the seal populations, though not to the same near-extinction slaughter level that the first Europeans achieved. Now they were protected and a tourist attraction; something for all passing motorists to spot in increasing numbers as the years went by.

With the sky and the sea lightning, I could see more and more of my surroundings. For fully three hours the road wound around the slowest and narrowest parts of the coast, the cliffs right to the sea and often necessitating tunnels to let the traffic flow smoothly. I counted more seals and myself lucky to be walking. At one stage I crossed a stony beach, mostly small black stones but a few very polished clear whites that I stopped to pick and have kept to this day.

For three hours I had dodged from side to side of the road, to give the motorists the best chance of avoiding me, so now I set off across the pebbly beach. The pebbles were tiny and crunchy but hard to walk on. Jim Wescomb contacted me by phone about the same time I was thinking about a crayfish lunch.

Kaikoura and its coast are renowned for what is a delicacy everywhere else but a must for all travelers. I was making good progress though and paused for the lunch, on what remained from the camping ground office, about seven miles from Kaikoura. A little closer to Kaikoura, I had my first experience of letting my pack go on ahead, after an offer from a young stranger. Many people stopped to offer me lifts and hitchhiking is still quite common in New Zealand. I always declined but this time, about eight kilometers (five miles) from my destination, I said that my pack would like a ride. Not being sure of where I was headed, I asked the kind young man, in a beat-up Ford Escort, to leave it at the first petrol station he came to.

The pack was there, of course. Does that seem too trusting? But given that someone is prepared to give me a lift without my asking, and given what Jesus said about going the extra mile, I was just acting out my Lord's instructions, and very pleased to be doing it.

I found my way into Kaikoura, dubbed the Whale Watching capital of New Zealand, teeming with tourists where once whalers and sealers had been the country's first European settlers, in the late 1700s and early 1800s. Times had changed, and the harpoons and salty tars of yesteryear had given way, to a whale-based tourist mecca. It's a town full of natural wonders, overlooked by majestic mountains, which are snow-capped for many months of the year. The combination of ocean and mountains offers stunning coastal alpine scenery and a host of eco-tourism activities, including whale watching and dolphin swimming. My walk along the coast showed me plenty of the latter, dolphins at play are a joy forever, as Keats said about things of beauty.

In the middle of the town, I found the Methodist pastor and his wife who were going to give me dinner and let me rest a bit. After my presentation in their small, but beautifully formed, church that evening, I was to go to the home of a senior member of the bible society. We got there just in time for the 7.30 p.m. start, so I had no time to make the acquaintance of my host for the night.

A small, enthusiastic crowd had gathered and we began. A sweet elderly lady was watching me intently from the front row but suddenly collapsed. I stopped speaking and people in the crowd went to her aid. She was lying flat on a pew and getting plenty of help when I took advantage of the hiatus to tell them I was staying with Alice that night and ask where she was. They pointed to the lady being treated and that brought a range of emotions, concern for her, of course, but just a little for myself. After a few minutes, she was well enough for me to continue but there was still concern for her, and once again the magnificence of the hospitality came to the fore as another couple offered to have me for the night.

Others offered to take my pack some of the way. I would meet them at my lunch stop the next day and they would carry the pack over the next hilly section. At the close of the day, now staying with hosts who stepped in at the last minute, I turned again to Jesus's journey.

"And he went forth again by the sea side; and all the multitude resorted unto him, and he taught them." Mark 2: 13 (KJV)

Jesus's visits to the lake shore, especially in Mark's gospel, are numerous. It almost seems he has a permanent platform, or maybe a soapbox, beside Lake Galilee. In this passage, He meets Levi (Matthew) and invites him to abandon his distasteful tax collecting. Then, in Mark 3, crowds come to him from all over the Holy Land, because they hear what He is doing (healing and preaching). In the same chapter, Jesus asks for a boat, to keep from being crushed and, in Mark 4, He uses an offshore boat to sit in and speak, while the large crowd listens on the beach. Sound carries farther over water than over land, especially over still water. Jesus had no amplification to get His message across to some very large crowds. He has only this adroit use of natural resources.

In Mark 5, we find Jesus on the shore again, and another large crowd gathering. This time He is with Jairus, the head of the synagogue, and the woman, who has been bleeding for twelve years, who touches Jesus's clothes for healing (before Jesus tells her faith made her whole). And, in Mark 6, Jesus feels sorry for a crowd that follows Him to a quiet place. He spends all day teaching them and then feeds them, all 5,000 men. Only Matthew of the other gospels mentions, "Besides women and children."

So, were there also women and children present? On one hand, it may be that only men were sufficiently interested, or permitted, to come and hear Jesus teach. On the other, many women were part of Jesus's entourage (for example, Mary Magdalene, Salome, and Mary the mother of James the Younger, as mentioned in Mark 15). It occurred to me, and I now suggest, tongue-in-cheek, that if women had been present beside the lake, the men would not have been without food. The same thing happens in Mark 8; a crowd on the shore forgets to bring food and Jesus feeds them, but this time it's a crowd of 4,000. Mark does not mention the location this time but says after the meal, Jesus and the disciples got into a boat, so it is by the lake.

Day Seven—Kaikoura to Conway (thirty-six kilometers or twenty-three miles)

Early away the next morning, I found the road continued to follow the coast for about sixteen kilometers (ten miles) and that was where I planned to stop for lunch and meet the kind people willing to take my pack over the Hunderlees, as the steep hilly section is known. They were to leave it with a farming family, where I would stay the night, though not perform Mark.

There were a few kilometers to walk through Kaikoura and I was on the road proper by 9 a.m., making a morning tea stop at the Cave Tearooms about an hour later. I recalled my first visit there. I was training to be a tour guide with the national bus tour company Trans Tours, a job that at age 20 I was lucky to have and one that gave me an excellent look at my own country before I did the inevitable Kiwi thing and went overseas for some Overseas Experience (OE) In my case, theatre training in Australia.

Now, at the Cave Tearooms on the outskirts of the town, I remembered the day bus trip from Christchurch to Kaikoura, which I took to observe a guide in action and during which I wondered how I would cope with such bus loads for weeks at a time. It was a very gentle assimilation and training period for me, looking back thirty-five years later.

The road flowed smoothly along the coast. I stopped to watch a motel have its façade redone and chat with the workers. Then I was alongside the sea again and in and out of the small tunnels on the coast. The adjacent railway, which competed with the road for the only space available between the cliffs and the sea, had more tunnels, but I avoided those. The roadside ones were tricky enough. It was past noon when I stopped at the tea rooms, and at about 1 p.m. my pack was collected. I set off for fifteen kilometers (nine and a half miles) of climbing and descending the windy road.

I had no cause for complaint, especially with the load off my back. The short afternoon passed, and the roadside counters told me I was making good progress. It was stunning scenery with the distant mountains leaning into the vistas of the pleasant tree-clad hills and with a light mist dancing over them all. And there was plenty of company, cows, and sheep in the fields and some lumbered by inside cattle wagons. In the main, New Zealand livestock do not winter indoors. The wool that is left on the sheep is enough to withstand the few falls of snow that are likely to appear at this latitude. So far, none on the journey, it was a dull greyish day and fading fast as the sunset hour of 5 p.m. approached. The hills were steep, and the sun was setting too fast. Now as the early twilight approached it was all downhill to the destination. No performance that night, but I had a welcome billet with a family who had farmed the surrounding land for three generations.

I had spoken to them before I left and learned that I would be an hour or so walking along their back boundary. It was getting darker now and I figured a kilometer or so to go. My usual method of counting posts told me it was a bit more. So, it would be truly dark before I reached the bridge and the turnoff to the homestead. A white van was ahead, and a gentle voice hailed me and offered me a ride. It was my hosts who asked if I had broken down. We laughed. I got in and they promised to drop me off at that point the next day. This was the second time that had to happen and not the last, but it was all part of my resolve that I would walk every inch of the South Island. What was the point otherwise?

I found that I had passed the back boundary of their large sheep farm an hour before, as the road continued easily downhill. Worried that I might be lost in the dark, they had come out a few minutes before. I found myself in the presence of an old established North Canterbury family. Several generations of them had settled the area and they were members of the congregation that I would have the pleasure of presenting Mark to the next evening. So, this was an evening off. Time to recoup and warm beside the fire, a genial meal where I learned their children were at boarding school in Christchurch and they were hunkered down for the winter. They lived near the banks of the Conway River, where my downhill route was leading, and their farm spread way into the hills. New Zealand being the small country it is, I discovered the family had had a hand in building a large railway viaduct near Taumarunui, the Makatote Viaduct no less, one of the many engineering feats that those 19th century pioneers tossed off with remarkable dexterity and left future generations to wonder over.

They left me with a book about the builder's exploits, from his arrival in a fledgling Christchurch, mostly swamp in the 1850s, and to that I turned as I took an early night. Ahead lay a decent walk, all of it with the pack, along the banks of the Conway River, which now murmured me to sleep.

Days One to Seven: 190 kilometers(120 miles). My maps
resemble treasure charts, of treasure in heaven.

CHAPTER THREE

Day Eight–Conway to Cheviot (thirty-one kilometers or nineteen miles)

WIDE AND BRAIDED, the Conway River that ruled this day was waiting for me when I woke up. I started from one and half kilometers (one mile) back up the road and approached the river with a certain stealth as if I was unsure I wanted it to be my companion for the distance that lay ahead. The walking was much easier than the night before and I soon had the backlog made up and swept alongside the now-welcoming river for the next few kilometers. There was just enough road shoulder to accommodate me, no rain and no hint of it; after all I had now crossed into Canterbury, the dry province, protected from the prevailing westerly by the Southern Alps.

It was a road I always enjoyed and today, with little hint of the coming winter storm, was especially pleasant. The road markers told me I was making good time, about 6 kph, (a bit slower than 4 mph pace) and a creditable feat with the pack. The road left the Conway, which now wanted to spurt into the brooding foothills of the Southern Alps in the distance and head for Parnassus where I intended to lunch. It was broad and easygoing, typical of the wide expanses of the South Island's main roads. But lunch was twenty kilometers (thirteen miles) distant and I trudged on.

Parnassus looked like a town that had seen a ghost, being too small to actually be a ghost town, thanks to a large road-cutting that took the speeding traffic past quickly on a new road that now missed the town by 400 meters. I was hungry so I went cross-country, for those 400 meters, and found the only place that was likely to provide a cup of tea and eats, the local garage and workshop. Everything was open as I walked in, but not a soul answered my call. The radio blared, the till stood temptingly by, and I walked round to the workshop at the back. Rousing someone in that place took a lot of work but finally, somebody came and found a cold meat pie for sale, which the microwave turned soggy, and a bottle of water. Quiet! It was surprising, in this island of 700,000 souls, most of them in the main cities, that this empty outpost even existed. A glance at the guidebook showed why. It noted that in 1914 the northbound rail route from Christchurch, 133km (80 miles) to the south struck construction problems at Parnassus and did not push on through those Hunderlees that I'd crossed the day before. I was not surprised. After World War I, the line bypassed Parnassus and took a coastal route to Kaikoura. So, the road by-pass was not the first time this sleepy little hamlet met the march of progress. The guidebook said I should investigate the remains of the abandoned railway and other local attractions.

Sadly, or rather thankfully, there was no time. But the wide, expansive skies were so attractive, especially as high, wide, grey clouds increased their intensity. It was on to Cheviot where a warm welcome, bed and performance of Mark awaited. No one who has travelled the South Island of New Zealand, especially in early winter, can get over the lack of vehicular traffic. This was the seventh day of my journey and curiously only one truck was aware of how far I'd come. As noted previously, every day, about thirty kilometers (twenty miles) further each day, the purple truck and trailer of the mail van would toot at me. The driver is still wondering about me, two decades plus later. Cheviot arrived with accompanying dusk and I found the tiny, quaint village which I had always only passed through. I was now in the Hurunui Valley and a pamphlet from the information center told me that Cheviot was the center of a pastoral farming area where visitors could enjoy coffee, or a meal at the cafes, or picnic at St Anne's Lagoon wildlife reserve with its English specimen trees. It said they can uncover stories in the museum, including those about a pioneer entrepreneur, Ready Money Robinson, whose historic homestead site at Cheviot Hills Reserve now includes a cricket ground, picnic areas, remnants of a colonial garden and walking track, sounds idyllic, I thought.

There was an historic Knox Presbyterian Church on the main road, but my presentation was at the Methodist Church, which was well attended. That was a credit to the local branch of the Bible society's members who came out despite the weather turning wetter and the wind more southerly. The branch was well led and warm to my task. Although the sanctuary was very cold, one small heater kept me warm, at least my feet, and they put on a great supper afterwards.

I stayed with a warm and comfortable retired pastor and his wife and the next morning, as rain threatened, he walked with me to the town's boundary, and we prayed beside the road for the success of my journey as my thoughts turned to Jesus's journey.

> "And it came to pass, that he went through the corn fields on the sabbath day; and his disciples began, as they went, to pluck the ears of corn. "Mark 2:23 (KJV)

> What looks like a simple walk through a wheat field is a greater journey for Jesus; one in which He directly challenges accepted teachings about keeping the Sabbath Day. While the disciples are husking the grain by rubbing it in their hands, Jesus is figuratively rubbing off the old thinking about for whom the Sabbath is made. The Pharisees say picking the grain in harvesting is work expressly forbidden on the Sabbath. Husking the grain is akin to threshing, also work forbidden on the Sabbath, they say.

> Branscomb notes the time and place are not specified, but that the grain is ripe and ready for harvest, so it must have been close to the Passover, and therefore at least a year before Jesus's arrival in Jerusalem, the week before the Passover of His crucifixion. For many, the time is not as important as Jesus's answer to the Pharisees. He uses the precedent of King David's hunger, referring to the time when David took, ate, and distributed the loaves only priests were supposed to eat. And he

concludes with an assertion that is bound to anger the Pharisees. "People are not made for the good of the Sabbath. The Sabbath is made for the good of people. So, the Son of Man is Lord over the Sabbath." After one of my performances of Mark, a woman in the audience demonstrated the technique of "hand-husking" and said she'd grown up in a wheat-growing country and all the kids in her family did it. I always imitate that rubbing and blowing in my performances now.

Day Nine—Cheviot to Greta Tavern (thirty-four kilometers or twenty-one miles)

It was blowing a southerly for the first time on the trip and rain not only threatened, it promised, in both the weather forecast and the skies above. My first hope was to reach Domett and have an early lunch before the rain came. This day was to be a hard slog into a head wind and driving rain, and little at the end of it but a hotel where there was, hopefully, some cheap accommodation, a warm fire and most importantly and likely, the televised rugby test from Wellington that evening.

With pack-a-back and the headstrong southerly, progress was slow on the gentle hills of North Canterbury, and I reached Domett about 10.30 a.m., even though the signposts said it was just seven kilometers (four miles) down the road. It was a lot more than that. The hamlet had seen better days. It was named after New Zealand's fourth premier, Alfred Domett, a friend of Robert Browning and Matthew Arnold in his youth and later a colonial administrator with a hardline on the native question. In other words, his treatment of the Māori people was harsher than they deserved. Now Domett was little more than a petrol station and an intriguing, converted railway station; the Mainline Station Café, which has since closed.

Once trains no longer stopped to give passengers refreshments, the café was relocated to the main road and was a very welcome stop for this pilgrim. The rest of the day is lost in a blur of fierce driving rain and the need to walk straight into it. Visibility dropped and I was lucky enough to find a metal reflector that had fallen onto the road somehow or another, about the size of a small shield. It did very well to make drivers aware of my presence. As the rain poured, the metal reflector kept some of it off me and picked up oncoming headlights. This kept up for several kilometers. I crossed the Hurunui River, another narrow South Island bridge that carried not a little danger, and climbed out the other side. After about three hours the rain seemed less and I struggled on, taking a meal/snack break under some covering trees. This was the first day of real rain but not the first I'd ever struck, and I had found some time back that I was not made of sugar and could handle a bit of rain; if the rain held a lesson it was that it too would pass, even cold, driving wind, though at this stage I had no idea how close the snow was behind.

It would be nice to report that I walked on through the storm with my head held high and singing hymns at the top of my voice, but my mind was in neutral as I tried to recall another time that I had made this journey in the rain. None came to mind although I must have traversed the road about 100 times, in daylight, at night, in my car, in others' cars, hitchhiking, buses, trains. All times had been dry.,

Then I remembered one particularly sodden journey. It did not come immediately to mind because I was going in the opposite direction. This one was from Christchurch to Picton on the morning of April 10, 1968. No New Zealander who lived through that day will forget it. It is now known as Wahine Day or the Day of the Wahine Storm.

TEV (turbo-electric vessel) Wahine was the Christchurch to Wellington vehicular overnight ferry, which alternated with *TEV Maori* making nightly journeys between the islands' main centers, Wellington and Christchurch.

The doomed vessel had left Christchurch on April 9, the Wednesday evening before Easter. Many college students were on it, but I was not one of them, though my mother, in the North Island, where I was heading for Easter, thought, in her pessimistic way, that I was.

Before dawn, on Maundy Thursday morning, the boat struck the brunt of a Cyclone Giselle, one of the worst ever to reach that far south, and was thrown onto Barrett Reef, near the entrance of Wellington Harbor. Rudderless and holed, it drifted into Wellington Harbor and sank within 200 meters off shore, at about 2 p.m. that afternoon. Of the 734 aboard, fifty-three lost their lives, drowned or died of injuries or exposure.

I heard the boat was aground on the early morning news, before I set off to hitchhike north in the teeth of the storm that was now heading south along the South Island's east coast. I reasoned that if the conditions were that bad, they were also likely to induce pity and therefore a ride.

And thus it transpired. I got one ride all the way to Picton. The driver and I heard on the car radio at 2 p.m, that the ship had capsized and all aboard were safe. We found that hard to believe, considering the elements that were now buffeting us. As we drove north, and as the storm drove south, we saw some of its wrecking power in the form of a caravan (trailer) that the wind had simply blown to small pieces, as its owners had towed it through a narrow cutting. When I got to Picton an hour or so after that evidence of nature's bitter fury, I learned all ferries were cancelled but I had no idea of the dramas across Cook Strait in Wellington. The Picton police let me stay in their old cells that night, not the ones with bars but an old block of unlocked rooms that served for such emergencies. It's probably long since torn down and turned into fancy motels.

About the middle of the afternoon, on my current walk into the wind and rain, my hosts from the Conway River stopped. They were coming back north from Christchurch where their son was at boarding school. They'd seen his rugby game and were heading home for warmth. They cheered me up with the news it was not far to go now, and nor was it.

I was in the Greta Tavern by 4 p.m. and beside the largest and most roaring fire I had ever seen. If I needed proof that nothing bad, uncomfortable or unsavory lasts forever, this was it. I found some cheap backpacker-type accommodation nearby, yes, they served meals, yes they were showing the test that evening, and yes this was the place to be. That fire roared as darkness and coziness fell. It kept roaring as the locals arrived to watch the game and nobody seemed to mind that it was going to be projected onto a sail they had rigged up in the bar. Nobody, least of all me. The locals roared at the game, England v New Zealand Maoris and even though it was relatively early when it finished, I went straight to bed, slept soundly in the small room with a heater provided, and woke to see snow on the ground; not much but enough to warn of what lay ahead.

Day Ten–Greta Tavern to Amberley (thirty-three kilometers or twenty miles)

The next day's assignment and I did not doubt that I would choose to accept, was to walk to Amberley, where I promised myself a motel to watch a semifinal of the World Cup (soccer/ football, depending on where you're from). There are many world cups, cricket and rugby being two that excite New Zealanders the most, but there is only one that galvanizes the whole world, and that evening the prospect of a warm motel with a television in the bedroom, a whole two stars more than last night, spurred me on, as all good ideas can.

There was snow on the ground, burst in from the south as I slept. I set off with some local advice, that the highest point on the road was not far ahead. It was Sunday morning, the second of my journey, but neither was there much time for church attendance. That was sad but true. I walked on and saw just a little snow that quickly melted with the morning sun. As I reached Omihi Pass, I met the spectacle of the great Canterbury Plains, my companion for many days ahead.

The foothills of the Southern Alps glistened in new-found winter splendor, proud to be snowclad mountains again and hoping to maintain their white coats until the spring thaw, while below them the green plains speckled with another white, the coats of many sheep for which Canterbury, province of my birth, is famous.

People who ask which island I am from usually get an oblique answer. I was born in Timaru, at the southern end of the plains that now ran into the distance for 260 kilometers (160 miles), but I was whisked away before I was two weeks old, to live in Whanganui, in the North Island. In those days, 1948, it was not expected or customary for a father to be present at childbirth. But I have often wondered what prompted my father to accept a new job in the North Island, pack up and take my two-year-old sister to her grandparents in Wellington then head off another 190 kilometers (120 miles) north, all with a pregnant wife still in Timaru. Was she too delicate to travel? Hardly. They were just different times.

About midmorning, a carload from my performance in Cheviot stopped and shared some small cakes and drinks with me. A gentle and enthusiastic woman was taking a team of young soccer players to another town and stopped for me on the way home. I reminded them of the World Cup soccer match that night.

After the pass, more like a gentle rise, it was indeed all downhill but nary a tearooms, so by the time I reached Waipara, where the road met the road to the West Coast, I needed refreshments. Waipara was another town devoted to the old railway days and after a stop at the local hotel, I headed for Amberley.

But time was getting on and I realized that I had ten kilometers (six miles) ahead of me and only an hour of light ahead of me. There was nothing wrong with that as I intended to backtrack the next day, as I had done twice before. The road climbed out of the Waipara River valley and passed a large winery.

A passer-by like me could see nothing strange in that; I assumed it was a wine-growing region, as had become increasingly obvious for the last few kilometers. But the young driver that gave me a ride shed new light on the district's history. He told me a cult called the Full Gospel Mission Fellowship was set up in the 1970s. In its heyday, it had several hundred followers, many of whom camped or were housed on the forty-hectare (one hundred-acre) site. The founder, Dr Doug Metcalf, who was later disgraced by allegations of adultery and died in 1989, bought the land in the 1970s for much less than it could fetch now, given its wine-producing qualities.

Some people were still living in the fort-like structure, though most had moved on, with some disillusionment and a desire end that chapter of their lives. Those who had left still held a stake in the property to which they had contributed all the cash they had earned, some for more than 20 years.

Later I investigated further and found newspaper accounts that told me armed men and women were prepared to fight in the 1970s for the survival of the camp. One, who is now a Presbyterian minister in the North Island, said people marched as a military group, basically preparing for, "What I consider was anarchy", he said. The minister, a 25-year-old flight crew member when he was introduced to the fellowship, was excommunicated in 1984, the first to be kicked out of the camp, after writing a 15-page thesis questioning the teachings and interpretation of scriptures at "Camp David". When they were evicted, he and his wife and two children "basically stepped out into a social vacuum," and many who followed over the years had struggled to "desocialize" themselves.

They found fellowship in the sect but there was a less desirable side to the Full Gospel Mission Fellowship. Women were the lesser creatures in more ways than one at the camp, and children were left to run riot as strict regimes of work and long scripture meetings most evenings took parents away for hours.

The camp rotated around an inner circle, that indoctrinated people to believe Dr. Metcalf was to be as revered as Jesus. They were thwarted by a police raid on the camp and members' homes throughout New Zealand in 1977. Firearms and ammunition were confiscated, and charges were laid against several sect members, including Dr. Metcalf. The charges were later dismissed. Police raided again in 1987, by which time a special "hit group" had been set up. However, a glitch with the search warrant gave members 48 hours to bury their arms.

As we drove the few miles to Amberley, with me searching for a motel with a television beside the bed – "Ah luxury!", I resolved to look at the Cooperites as he called them a little closer. Nothing on the surface of the green and pleasant, even in winter, land, gave any indication that things were not as they should have been. Grapes were obviously the "in" thing now, but not the grapes of wrath. Communes and communal living were a way of life in New Zealand in the 1970s and gained a measure of Government support with the Ohu schemes promoted by the socialist-leaning Labour Government of 1972-75.

For the record the match I watched in Amberley was Spain v Ireland and, being one-quarter Irish, it was very important, or it took on a greater degree of importance than it needed to. Spain won in a penalty shoot-out 3-2, and I slept warm and well, planning to hitchhike back to Waipara before starting the journey again.

Day Eleven—Amberley to Rangiora (twenty-six kilometers or sixteen miles)

I rose early and breakfasted at a café in the little town and hitchhiked to my starting point, ten kilometers (six miles) to the north. A ride came in no time at all, and here was more evidence that hitchhiking is still an accepted form of transportation in New Zealand, one that I would rely on several times on this trip. Its general acceptance is despite a few well-publicized cases of women going missing while hitching. Most people understood that women hitchhiking alone were being a little irresponsible, but solo men were fine. That's unfair, of course, but it is a matter of combining trust with commonsense. I used the mode twice on this leg of the journey, a total of twenty kilometers (twelve miles) and a few days later, again about 20km. A total of forty kilometers, all of them freely given.

Those who condemn hitchhiking as bludging, cadging, and getting a free ride have probably never hitched nor offered a ride. Having done it often in my youth I have resolved to always pick up hitchhikers myself and never to judge those who do not. As a hitchhiker I would always give a driver who failed to stop a cheery wave anyway; that attitude got me at least one lift, from the driver who saw me wave, realized I was a friendly guy and stopped although he had not meant to. In my youth, a friend picked up a hitchhiker and brought him back to our student flat, and established a friendship that resonated in my life so deeply that it took me to Adelaide for two years, where I discovered my acting talents and set off on the path that brought me to this spot. Nothing happens by chance unless you ignore it. There is a deep Christian message of acceptance there.

My ride was a young man going to work in one of the near-Waipara vineyards and he was intrigued to hear about my journey. Snow lay around the railway tracks on the side of the road, as I turned my head again south and set off again for Amberley, which I planned to reach about 10:30 a.m. (AGW – All Going Well). My contact with the Bible Society in the top half of the South Island, Jim Wescomb, was to meet me in Amberley and take the pack, still sitting at the motel, with him to our destination in Rangiora. This was going to be a packless day but not, however, a snowless day, as the glowering skies forecast.

The wind got up as I reached Amberley, and my cell phone rang. It was the other Bible society contact, Margaret Black, calling from Dunedin, to welcome me to her territory. I still had some of Jim's region to traverse but was delighted to hear from her. At Amberley, I had thirty kilometers (eighteen miles) to go and without a pack that was going to be easy. But the wind was whipping up, the rain more threatening and turning a nasty sleetish cold.

Jim pulled alongside. His cheery burr, an accent from New Zealand's deep south, was as encouraging as the sky was daunting. We shared a little lunch and he reminded me that the residents of Rangiora were looking forward to hearing Mark that evening. I did not want to wait around as the rain was getting heavier and he offered a slight temptation, knowing I would decline, of a lift. Jim had been a sturdy sheep farmer in Southland and he'd seen far worse than this, been in much worse too.

Still, he expressed admiration for my efforts and I plugged on, admiring the little town of Balcairn, just one of the many towns, once tiny and now minuscule, that attest to New Zealand's population drift north over the last 100 years. It was curious that as my walk south progressed, I saw evidence that same drift grew more pronounced. I was in the Kowai District of the sparsely populated North Canterbury and the architecture reflected it. It comprised a series of uncharacteristically ornate, albeit wooden, buildings spread around in an area that hardly seemed big enough to support them.

Since 1875, The Kowai District Council offices in Balcairn have been a center for local body activities. That building is the home of the Kowai-Sefton Archives Group which restored the site in 1995. Since it is more a collection of archives than a museum, it houses many of the local school and church records of the area. The building, with a Historical Places Trust grade 2, was built in 1922 as a Peace Memorial and has an impressive memorial plaque.

Thoughts of the population that had passed spurred me on a little, but the wind became more biting and, as the road turned westward, the rain followed and now drove into my face with increasing cold. At Sefton I found a gas station and a sign that promised me rest in Rangiora, now twelve kilometers (eight miles) away. That's a lot of rain and pre-snow to get through. I was well-protected, with a warm hat and coat over my long trousers and a raincoat and gloves that kept out most of the cold, but as the rain drove in, the trousers soaked and shorts would have been more practical. Frankly, a full-length clear plastic rubbish bag would have been best of all.

It was a secondary highway and therefore lacked many vehicles. I found bigger trucks were the most menace on rainy days, because they threw up sheets of water about two meters on either side of them. I could dodge them by retreating off the road but that slowed my progress if I was forever skipping sideways into ditches. But on this early afternoon I trudged on and in the interest of getting to my journey's end quickly, took several drenchings from passing trucks head-on, only skipping a meter sideways as each wave washed me.

The wind drove harder and colder and I was delighted to finally reach the outskirts of Rangiora, the biggest town in those parts, and Jim's home and my rest for the night. I rang him from the shelter of a tree to get directions and this time his persuading struck home. We agreed I had reached Rangiora, and riding a few hundred meters, the lift he was trying to offer, would not harm the integrity of the walk. Jim picked me up, now freezing and sodden, and took me home. It was about 4 p.m. and I went straight into a warm shower. I shivered there too, and it was fully five minutes before I realized I was standing under a hot shower, and not the freezing rain that had numbed my brain.

A fire roared, as others did at every stop in the South Island from that day, for that day it snowed. In my case, the snow came down about 5 p.m., about an hour before we drove to the church for our evening performance that was going to be preceded by an evening meal.

Jim expected it would keep many people away. Quite a few lived in the country and would not like to venture out in fresh snow, and all the uncertainties involved. So it proved. The twenty-five hardy souls that did come out in the falling snow were delighted to hear Mark's gospel and I was thrilled to give it to them. Never once did I stop and think about how many could have come. It has never been my habit to blame a small audience, and I would tell any other actors, complaining about a small house, that those who had come were going against the trend, as it were, and were more deserving of a good performance because they had made the extra effort. Those people of Rangiora, on June 17, 2002, deserved every bit as much if not more, of the good news than those who stayed away. That evening my thoughts turned with gratitude to Jesus's journey.

> "And he goeth up into a mountain, and calleth unto him whom he would: and they came unto him" Mark 3:13 (KJV)

> Jesus's walk up the mountain to select his disciples is a step towards expanding His, at this stage, local mission. The mountain's name is not significant. It was just a place away from the crowds where He would call more than twelve to come with Him before making his choice. So, what about those not selected for his inner circle? They would be disappointed, watching their friends being selected and realizing Jesus was not going to pick them. This is not like not being chosen for a pickup game, or not getting a promotion; this is huge, the chance to become, as Jesus had promised, fishers of men. For those chosen, it was the start of a journey that gave them the chance to be close to Jesus, and one which I suggest parallels my walk. This was the first time Jesus delegated healing and spiritual power, and authority. But for those who missed out, it must have been a sad, lonely walk back down the mountain.

Day Twelve–Rangiora to Kaiapoi (ten kilometers or six miles)

Jim Wescomb farewelled me the next morning and I trudged through a snowclad Rangiora. Ahead lay Christchurch and two performances, one in an Anglican church the next afternoon and the other the following evening. The second would be special, hosted by Jim Stuart who first encouraged me to do Mark's gospel early in 2000, and who had since moved to a Methodist church in Christchurch's suburbs.

The first time I saw Christchurch it was snowing; the winter of 1967 and I was eighteen years old. I had walked around that city all night, thrilled with the sight of snow falling on empty streets. I did not sleep that night. I walked from the city to the new Ilam campus and savored my recent good fortune, of being selected for the final of a quiz show. Such is the energy of youth.

So, I was going to come back the next week, at my own expense. Back in 1967, there was no real glamor attached to a nightly quiz show in the tent of a winter show, the August equivalent of the summer show but inside, mostly. I was excited about possibly winning the prize, a trip to Australia, and just walked around the streets. The small hours came and I kept walking. About 5 a.m., a cop pulled over to check me out and I explained that it was my first visit to the big city and that I wanted to see all I could in the limited time available. I was wearing my ubiquitous black duffel coat with the red lining that my stepmother, Jean Darling had sewed in, with more love than ability. She knew I wanted something resembling a magician's coat to make my mark in my first year of college and tacked in the red satin lining. I was also wearing an astrakhan Russian hat that I bought with an equal flourish a few weeks before, as winter set in. The hat and I and parted company when it chose to stay in the back seat of the car that took me back north the next day. I slept in the car most of the way to Picton after being awake all the previous night. That's just one memory of snow and Christchurch on my journey that brought back into sharp relief a life lived owing many thanks to many.

But more immediately lay the crisp and clean little town of Rangiora. Sun shone at first and I made a good start, in time to see the children going to school, mostly on foot, even in the light snow that had fallen. After about two kilometers, the sun went behind clouds that foretold more rain and after five kilometers (three miles), still walking toward Christchurch, the cold rain drove in. I hooded up and kept walking, my pack getting a little more soaked than I and after half an hour I was so much of a bedraggled mess that a young woman, with a small child on board, offered me a ride. I demurred but she insisted. I looked around for a landmark, to remember where I would resume my journey. It was close to Kaiapoi. Then I accepted her offer with great relief and the rain pelted down. It was a unique experience for me, getting into a car with a young woman and child, determined to give me a ride. She just said quietly, when I initially refused her offer to get in, "I think you should."

I could not argue against that quiet insistence, and as I got in, I could not help thinking how strong the possibility was she had been sent, just one of the many on the road who got me from one end of the South Island to the other. Of course, she was sent. She gave with love.

We reached the suburbs of Christchurch and the day grew greyer and more miserable, the rain clearing out snow that falls about three times a year on the Canterbury capital. Christchurch's population is 350,000 give or take and has 2,100 hours of sunshine but none on this winter day. It looked as though we would go below the mean annual minimum temperature of 1C (34F). There are eighty-five days a year when 1mm (1/16th of an inch) or more of rain falls and this was certainly one of them. It was a cold and grey Cathedral Square that I reached by public transport and after buying gloves at a department store, found my cousin who was putting me up for the next two nights.

Day Thirteen–In Christchurch (resting feet)

Mark was due to appear at St Peter's Church, in the suburb of Upper Riccarton, the next afternoon and I found it, with the help of the excellent public transport, on the corner of the Yaldhurst and Main South roads. I had time to explore its surroundings. It had one of the oldest cemeteries in Christchurch, dating from 1857. The first wooden church on the property was built and consecrated in 1858. It was enlarged in stone and brick in 1901 and 1928 and has some rare and beautiful stained-glass windows.

At 2 p.m. the throng of matinee goers arrived, mostly elderly women and totally attentive. This was my only afternoon presentation of Mark's gospel and the experiment worked very well. I used the front of the nave to move around, and they were engrossed and said how much they'd enjoyed themselves. Christchurch has often been called "more English than the English" and there is a hint about the place that this is a transplanted middle-class England, especially when the Anglican Church is given such a prominent place. It has always been like that. The settlers in the 1850s, from the "First Four Ships" made sure of it. It was a Church of England settlement and as proud then as it is now of that heritage. So, it was a gentle hearing Mark got, a dignified and gentle hearing and a rewarding one for us all. And, as my custom was after every performance, my prayers of gratitude turned to Jesus and His journey.

> "And the same day, when the even was come, he saith unto them, Let us pass over unto the other side." Mark 4:35 (KJV)

> It may seem more but in this gospel, Jesus crosses the lake six times. The first is in Mark 4 when He calms the wind and the waves and comes ashore near Gerasa, where he meets the man infested with evil spirits. The second is soon after, when He sends the evil spirits into 2,000 pigs, is asked to leave that part of the country, and must cross again. The third occasion is just before feeding the 5,000 and the fourth immediately after, when the disciples row across toward Bethsaida and Jesus walks on water to catch up with them. Mark records that the voyage makes landfall at Gennesaret. In Mark 8, Jesus and the disciples cross for the fifth time, after feeding the 4,000, to Dalmanutha. They stay there briefly (just verse 12) and return after a short discussion with the Pharisees That's the sixth crossing Mark records.

After the performance, I had time for a quick drink in a hotel with an old theatre friend who quickly admitted he was quite nervous about meeting me after nearly thirty years, especially as I was doing Mark's gospel and he thought I must have "got religion" or something else equally dreadful. Those fears fell away just as quickly and we laughed and joked about the time we had spent together acting at the professional theatre in Whanganui. We did at least four plays together including one where I was cast as a gay actor from New York and he was a Vietnam War veteran, in the classic *Kennedy's Children*. We thought we'd get the other's part and he was impressed with my depiction of Sparger as a person first, an actor second and gay third. Graham admitted he'd have gone for the camp laughs. We worked on a magical children's play *The Nobodies from Nowwhere,* which required absolute concentration and truth in performance on the actor's part, because we were acting for children. As the saying goes, "How do you act for children?" The answer is, "The same as for adults, only better." Children are quicker to seize on lackadaisical acting. They are genuine in their expectations, and less forgiving when an actor underperforms. A patron in the bar stopped to ask Graham if he was still acting as the chairperson in Olde Time Musical. Graham made a straight reply and when the man had gone gave a camp sigh, "I still have a public."

Day Fourteen–In Christchurch (resting feet)

The next day I again used public transport, to get myself to Jim and Gillian's house where I was eagerly awaited. It was the first time I had seen them since 2000 and they told me their congregation was also eager to hear me. We dined and listened to Jim's incredible learning, knowledge and wisdom before setting out for their church nearby.

An audience member asked me if a young South Korean woman, who was going to be in the front row, could follow the performance from the "script". Her English was not too good, she explained, and of course I agreed. It was nice to be asked.

Jim and Gillian sat near the back and I was glad they could hear Mark again. I always think of Gillian when I come to the line in Chapter 1, about bringing people instead of fish. When she had first heard me practicing it, Gillian said she was disappointed. She liked the King James version, "Fishers of men," and I did too. So, when I come to that passage I think of her.

Jim said they knew the audience was with me when they heard someone in front of them whispering to themselves, "Shall be last" when I came to the passage "Those who are first, etc." Jesus's journey, not my own, was again to the fore, because without His, mine would not be possible.

> "And he went out from thence, and came into his own country; and his disciples follow him And when the sabbath day was come, he began to teach in the synagogue: and many hearing him were astonished, saying, From whence hath this man these things? and

what wisdom is this which is given unto him, that even such mighty works are wrought by his hands? "Mark 6:1-2 (KJV)

Jesus begins a journey of acceptance by His own people, one in which He knows He will fail. And He knows why. He knows that familiarity breeds, if not contempt, then a certain amount of over-familiarity. So, He explains the opposition to His teaching saying that a prophet was not without honor, except in his native place and his own home. It appears, from Mark's account, that Jesus family did not try to counter the skepticism of the people of Nazareth, yet the book of Acts shows they remained loyal to His teaching and were leaders in the early church, especially His brother James, who headed the Jerusalem Church.

Even so, it is interesting Jesus does not take His mission to his hometown before He's spoken all over Galilee. He knows the reception his message would get; though Mark reports that while people are amazed at His teaching, they wonder where His wisdom comes from, knowing His origins as a carpenter.

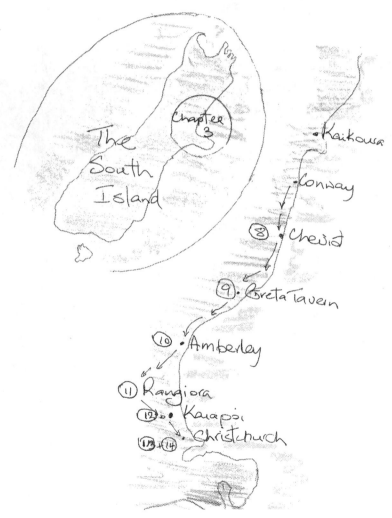

Days eight to fourteen: 134 kilometers (82 miles)

CHAPTER FOUR

Day Fifteen–Kaiapoi to Hornby (twenty-five kilometers or sixteen miles)

IT WAS GREY, and threatening rain, the next morning, when Jim Stuart drove me to the spot where I'd been rescued from more rain. All this backtracking was becoming a bit of a saga but reminded myself that I had not put my thumb up. The young woman had insisted I get into her car to escape the driving rain.

We drove to where she had picked me up and then Jim drove my pack across Christchurch to where I figured I could reach that night, the camping ground in Hornby. It would have a cabin available. I was going to cut across and around Christchurch, as any traveler, wanting to bypass the big city, would. And it was a long day through the suburbs, peppered with stops to buy a woolen hat and get warm in lunch stops, afternoon tea stops, and finally dinner stops, all the time knowing the faithful Jim had taken my pack on ahead. The camping ground where I found the pack was very basic and the small cabin I rented was not much to write home about. It had just a small heater to fend off the cold and bring a lot of needed sleep.

Day Sixteen–Hornby to Dunsandel (thirty-one kilometers or nineteen miles)

The next morning, I struggled to find the motivation to get up. As I lay half awake, I realized that ahead lay two days without performances. After Jim's in Christchurch, I had three days of walking before the next, but that was par for the course on an island the size of New Zealand's

South, which boasted just 700,000 in the whole island and half of those in Christchurch.

So, it was more walking through the suburbs. The first stop was breakfast at McDonalds and then the road started to get very flat, straight, and daunting. I found a meal in the Rolleston hotel on the side of the road but it was a very late lunch and despite a hard afternoon slog, by the time I reached Dunsandel in low late-afternoon light, I still had seventeen kilometers (eleven miles) before Rakaia, where I had booked a room at St Ida's Guest House, and where I planned to watch a rugby match between New Zealand and Australia.

The day closed in, a very early dusk falling. It was obvious I would never make it, the effort of having to play catch-up from Kaiapoi to Christchurch, two days before, was taking its toll and I was seriously behind the eight ball. I put my thumb up again. I got a ride almost straight away, and arrived in Rakaia just before dark set in irrevocably.

What a pleasant town! St Ida's guest house had been the local catholic school and convent. For just $60, it's probably gone up just slightly in the last two decades, I found an ensuite bathroom, a superb breakfast the next day, and genial hosts in Ken and Miriam Cutforth, who had a great fire going in anticipation of a warm night watching a rugby international.

Day Seventeen—Dunsandel to Ashburton (forty-six kilometers or twenty-nine miles)

On this Sunday I walked more than a marathon. First, seventeen kilometers before breakfast, without a pack and, after breakfast in Rakaia, another twenty-eight with the heavy pack to Ashburton. I performed to 200 people and had my prayers answered.

The day began long before dawn, at 6 a.m. I had still not conquered the long straights of the Canterbury Plains, nor the darkness in midwinter. Ken, my host dropped me off from where I'd hitched a ride from the night before. It was a relatively short drive back north but there was no compromising. If I wanted to say, unequivocally, without contradiction, even by myself, that I'd walked the South Island, I had to go back to where I started.

It was freezing cold. Snow lay piled in drifts from the fall three days before, and this snow I was to see for the next few days despite fine weather. We figured I'd be back in about three hours, and I noticed as I got the sleep out of my head that this was a very long straight by New Zealand standards. Ken was used to early rises. The life of a bed-and-breakfast husband and wife meant making exactly that, but not in that order. First came the breakfast for the handful of guests, then the beds. The rest of the day was their own.

What motivated this man to rise even earlier than usual to get me back to my breaking off/starting point? The price of the accommodation was a simple, almost paltry, $60. At that rate, he and his wife were battling. I learned later he also sold real estate and gave some fine, uncompromising South Island hospitality. Doubtless, he'd done the same and more many times, and his "going the extra mile" was not the first on that eventful journey, a Christian act without even stopping to think about it. He was just happy to be part of the adventure.

He dropped me off, about 6.15 a.m. and I watched his red tail lights disappear as he drove back to Rakaia. They shone for at least five minutes. Well-wrapped, I set off after them without any idea how fast I was going, I set a steady pace nevertheless, in the pitch darkness. I used my torch (flashlight) to highlight my position to oncoming motorists.

With little wind and the promise of a clear morning, I soon saw a white light ahead and knew it was an oncoming car. What else could it be, unless it was the train on the tracks that ran parallel to the road? This was the South Island main highway, and there was just one car on it about ten kilometers (six miles) away. I counted a full five minutes before that light, running towards me at 100 kph (60 mph) or more, became two headlights, grew larger, and then whizzed past. The mathematics were easier in imperial measures. A car traveling for five minutes (one twelfth of an hour) at 60 mph will cover what distance? Sixty divided by twelve = five. So, that meant there were five miles of straight road ahead because that is how far away the car was when it first appeared.

I kept on at pace Without a pack on me, or breakfast inside me, it was easy to walk quickly, about 4 mph. That meant I would get around the bend in about seventy-five minutes, but there was no way to tell how fast I was doing. All was relative to the dark and the still early morning.

Soon lights began to take four and a half minutes to reach me, then four, and still the dawn refused to arrive. I was warm enough and the lights when they appeared were closing in on me at shorter and shorter intervals. But always just the single light, still too far off to appear as two. Well, you can draw an allegory from that if you like. I was just happy to draw nearer to breakfast.

The first time I drove on this stretch was the first time I drove, aged eighteen. Well, I'd had a few lessons, but I was hardly ready for the unnerving stint behind the wheel of Jim McKenzie's Austin A40 on a winter's evening. On and on and on that road went, and the effort to steer straight, which I'd not yet naturally learned, was enormous.

I had much more fun a year later, again in winter, when I drove another old Austin, David Wickham's A40 Countryman, a vehicle he called his "three-liter mass-o-rattles", to Dunedin in the middle of the night.

That time, I'd only come to keep him awake but he fell asleep about twenty kilometers (twelve miles) into the journey, or rather the car slowed, and I realized that if we were going any further, I'd be driving, still without a license, to Dunedin. Some journeys are a watershed, and this was one of them. These days, in modern cars, the Christchurch-Dunedin journey takes about five hours. This was longer. Hampered by a headwind, the mass-o-rattles rarely went faster than 80 kph (50 mph). We froze without an adequate heater, but Wick slept through it. We stopped once, about 3 a.m. in Timaru, and found no friendly all-night gas station in 1969, just a lone pint of milk on the steps of an office building, cold and feloniously obtained. Wick slept on as Dunedin and the reason for our journey approached. The city was snowed in, and we'd wanted to see it and be part of it. Chains were needed on the hills north of the city and high crosswinds blew us out of our lane as we approached. The southern city in the pre-dawn looked like a Christmas Card.

Bang on 7 a.m. and eight hours since we left Christchurch, we knocked on the door of student friends from high school, the light just strong enough to see the remains of a snowman in the front yard, which they'd made the day before. They were as amazed as we hoped they would be, but Wick rained on the parade a little by announcing he was staying a few days.

But I had to be on stage that night! I thought we were turning round and driving straight back, that's why I came. I was in what was to become a legendary production of *A Midsummer Night's Dream*, directed by Dame Ngaio Marsh, for the Canterbury University Drama Society.

Until I got my final ride, from Timaru to Christchurch about 3 p.m., I was a nervous wreck wondering how the other actors would handle me being stuck in Dunedin? Here is why the journey became a watershed. I got back in good time, hitchhiking naturally, and Wick returned a few days later with a hitchhiker of his own. John was an Australian paua shell diver (but later admitted he was taking a break from being an accountant in Adelaide) who worked in Invercargill, at the bottom of the South Island, where my walk was taking me. He had a girlfriend in Christchurch, and would come to visit often in the next few months. A year later, I was staying with him in Adelaide where we flatted together for two years, and where I studied theatre. Had it not been for John I would not have gone to Adelaide and been told I had a bright future as an actor, and that I would be a lost soul all my life if I did not make theatre my life. The question then and now, was how to combine theatre and the worship of God. "Do Mark," was, and still is, the answer.

Rakaia drew nearer as the night turned to day but there was one obstacle left. The one and a half kilometers (one mile) length of road bridge is very narrow. It's also the longest bridge in the national roading network. The Rakaia is a braided river, and its changing channels spread over a wide area. In normal flows, the braided river channels sweep in winding courses across the gravel beds. which are up to a mile wide. During spring and summer floods, fed by the melting snow, the waters reach from bank to bank, so long multi-span structures are needed.

Because of its climate and topography, New Zealand has more bridges, on a population basis, than any other country in the world. An early solution to the cost problem was to build a bridge both rail and road traffic would use. But that was in 1873. In 1939 they opened a road bridge alongside the present rail bridge and took away the now unnecessary road part.

I decided to go inland 200 meters, upstream from the road, and take the rail bridge for the long crossing. Goods trains did not run on Sundays in the South Island and no passenger trains ran farther south than Christchurch. The glamor of rail travel that enthralls Europe and its large population does not excite tourists and certainly not the native population.

Travelers who zoom across the road bridge miss something special and the word should get out, that a Sunday morning walk across the bridge, with no fear of a train coming, is an ideal jaunt for the locals. An excursion train might come, but that's where faith, and the emergency laybys, come in.

It was a glorious walk in the early morning; the snow drifts on the sides of the road behind me gave way to mountains reaching almost to the river in the distance as I looked upstream. Below me the classic pale blue of the South Island glacial-melt river and braids sweeping and turning as they formed their course. By contrast, mine was right ahead and I clipped along happily, savoring the moment that the mountains put their winter coat on against the clear blue of the still Sunday morning. I reached the guest house again at 9.30 a.m. and found a late breakfast waiting so it was not much before 11 a.m. that I set off for Ashburton, pack-a-back and already seventeen kilometers under my belt with another thirty kilometers (nineteen miles) to go.

At my pack-carrying pace, I was looking at a 5 p.m. arrival in Ashburton and I tried hard to keep a steady rhythm for my feet. It was flat and easy walking, but my feet were getting sore. The organizers of the gospel presentation that evening did their best to encourage me by cell phone, and the local press came out to meet me, take a picture, and leave me to it. And still I walked on, trying to ignore sorer and sorer feet. With not many places to find a drink, I sipped at my meager supply of water.

Sore feet on the march was my first physical trouble. No sore knees or back, and least of all feet, until now. I think the new trainers were the problem, rubbing hard against my heels. I was still striding along but giving a few limping moments when I young man pulled up alongside me.

"Are you Geoffrey? I am coming to hear you tonight."

"Great," I said and of course I added, "How far to go?"

"About five miles now. God has told me to pray for your feet. Get in."

Although this was the main highway (Route 1) it was only one lane wide in either direction. He was almost close enough to touch as he pulled alongside, and I took the pack off and hobbled across to him.

We prayed then and there, in the front seat, for the Lord to bless my sore feet, to give me purpose, and reach my destination safely. It was a simple and loving act and when I raised my head, I felt lighter and younger and my feet had no pain. I skipped across the road, back to my pack, and set off again, renewed and thanking the Lord for sending me one of His faithful servants.

Soon the Ashburton organizer arrived with another drink, and I kept going as night closed, just before the town of Ashburton hove into view, as sailors don't say. At my hosts' house, they gave me a warm bath and a little rest, some methylated spirits for my feet, and the opportunity to savor my longest day, forty-five and half kilometers (twenty-nine miles) and the majority with a pack. A marathon indeed.

I presented Mark in bare feet that evening and later several members of the audience said they could see the blisters. One man stopped me in the street the next day, as I was walking out of Ashburton, and told me I had been limping so badly he wanted to offer me a lift. Bless him.

There were about 120 people who heard Mark's gospel presented after that marathon day and there was no better reconstruction of how the gospel was first brought to people, not only all over the Middle East but all over the world, by people walking and using word of mouth. That is why it was disappointing that one young woman chose to sit near the front and follow along with an open Bible. I had asked that this practice be discouraged but it is hard when the habit, at regular church services, of reading along with the lesson reader is ingrained, even encouraged. We got along fine until I made a slight mistake and noticed her smirk. I bristled a bit inside, thinking the one thing I did not need at the end of a long day was a triumphant smirk.

I made an excuse, took a break, and asked for someone to ask her to stop. The pastor said he'd deal with it, but she was still there smirking at every slight mistake. The more I tried to avoid them the more they came; but after the many performances I was able to get through the marathon day by the simple act of forgiving the girl, she did not know what she was doing. No doubt she thought she was a superior being for having become a Christian, and that showed in every smirk, but she had a lot to learn and a lot to go through before she truly walked with Jesus. Nobody knew how much she unsettled me, until now. Her attitude was so disappointing. But for the organizers it was a triumph; In Ashburton, the Word lived. And that night I again turned my mind to Jesus's journey.

> "And he called unto him the twelve, and began to send them forth by two and two; and gave them power over unclean spirits; And commanded them that they should take nothing for their journey, save a staff only; no scrip, no bread, no money in their purse. But be shod with sandals; and not put on two coats." Mark 6:7-9 (KJV)

This is classic advice for a journey, the ultimate "travel light", and, interestingly, Jesus chooses the end of His visit to Nazareth to send out the first "missionaries". Perhaps He is showing his hometown how serious and committed His followers are. Walking any distance without food, a bag, or money must be the ultimate test of faith and dedication. My walk down the South Island demonstrated to me, and to others I met, the significance of Jesus's instructions. It's all about the journey. In preparing for a journey, we try to pack as lightly as possible but always end up taking too much. If we travel as lightly as Jesus asked his disciples to, we'd acknowledge that journeys are not about carrying stuff with us. They are about the journey itself, the messages we spread, and the people we meet.

And Jesus's giving the twelve power over evil spirits is all the protection they need (and the sandals and the walking stick which He allows). Luke 10 talks about many more of Jesus's followers, 70 in fact, going out in groups of two, and returning rejoicing over the evil spirits that bowed to Jesus's name. In Mark, there is also a debriefing passage, when the disciples gather around Jesus to tell Him all they have taught and done. But so many others make demands of Jesus's time that he suggests withdrawal to a quiet place, which begins the miracle of feeding of the 5,000.

Day Eighteen–Ashburton to Rangitata (thirty-five kilometers or twenty-two miles)

The humble crosses everywhere
Mark the passing souls
Who drove this road with little care,
And never reached their goals.

A walk the length of the South Island gives time to pause at every roadside cross, something few motorists ever do. Early in the journey I jotted down the wayside epitaphs. And here are a few that I, as a walker, was privileged to record and contemplate. Everyone else whirls past without time to read or reflect on the lives so suddenly ended.

Darren, only dead flowers to be seen at 4.15 p.m., en route to Geraldine.

Graham Thomas Johns, and a handful of faded artificial flowers. I wondered:

Did you know young Graham Thomas Johns
That the moment had come when you would be gone?

Dale Lincoln Williams:
July 1, 1980 – December 4, 2001.
That was simply put and it tells of a tragic Christmas for a family still coming to terms with the sudden loss of such a young life.

Like this one – No name – just an Indian amulet and plastic flowers.

Then, "Georgie (April 2, 1991- September 2, 2001)"
With the picture of a dog that I guessed was killed on the corner.

Of this one, there is no doubt: A picture of a smiling and vibrant young woman aged early thirties: "Her life's an inspiration to all who have been blessed by her friendship. A woman of excellence." Her plaque nestled within the willows, and no hint remained that a terrible crash had once happened at this picturesque spot.

Such pauses on the journey gave me time to reflect on the waste of life, just as we reflect on the waste of money that goes hand in hand with such personalized plates as WOTZUP. As I left Ashburton, I noticed a good one - GR8D4Y – Great Day, of course. But what a waste! That number plate cost $350, money that could have gone to a million charities. Surely it's more important to give money than to waste it on such plates, also called Vanity Plates, for obvious reasons.

When Jesus rebuked his disciples, who said perfume spilled on his head could have been sold for 300 silver coins and the money given to the poor, he was making the point that He would not always be with them; and the secondary point that the woman showed great devotion and was preparing His body for burial. There is no such message in people adorning their pride and joys with such inanities as NOT 4U or PAID 4.

I find in my diary that I left Ashburton at 10.40 a.m., with flat, wide, and straight roads to accompany me to Hinds, twelve kilometers (eight miles) away, where I expected to have lunch. How could it have been so late? I had gone slowly out of town, taking in the beauty of the recent snowfall and the many old churches that depicted a larger town than Ashburton was now. The further south I went, the more relics of a very established post-pioneer New Zealand there seemed to be. It was fine again and would remain so for several days. I was warm and optimistic about getting to Hinds before too much hunger set in.

Although I reflected on the waste, I also reflected on the wonderful generosity of people like those I had stayed with. That morning they had offered me the use of their cabin in the Peel Forest nearby if I wanted to stop there and write up my thoughts and memories of the trip. Then my pack was carried ahead, and I planned to pick it up at Hinds, but that afternoon, as I battled with the long straights and the need to keep going on newly-hardened blisters, my host returned from his trip south and announced he had, "Gone the extra mile," and taken my pack to Rangitata, where my journey that day would end. He brought some drink and a small snack, and both were very welcome; we parted after a short prayer for my journey and his continued health and carried on towards Hinds.

I was now sixteen days into the journey and I was enjoying it very much now the blisters had hardened. I remembered a game I'd played years ago, based on cricket and the number plates of cars. As I strode along, I counted the last number on every car. If it were a six, that many runs were scored. If it was a nine, then the combined total was fifteen, and so on. If that last number were zero, then the batsman was out and another would take his place until all eleven had batted. This way, an hour or so could pass. That might seem odd, that I was not constantly filled with thoughts of a higher power, as I strove to do His work.

That afternoon allowed a full-scale match in which one player scored 109 and several got no score, ducks, zilch, nyet, nada, as two cars in succession passed with their last numbers zero. Precious little else occurred as the day wore on. Onwards went the road, the kilometers/miles counting down with the aid of the markers, and I kept up a steady pace. Few cars passed, in either direction, and as dusk neared, I realized I would reach the next braided river, the Rangitata and its accompanying narrow bridge, with certainly no footpath or walkway, when it was already dark.

I was going to branch off to Geraldine that evening and a teacher who lived in that inland town was coming from further north, behind me, to pick me up. We expected to rendezvous at Rangitata. That was thirty- five kilometers (twenty-two miles) in the day and not bad going for such a late start, though without a pack. The sunset was glorious, a treasured memory, but after sunset comes the dark, so I pressed on. The bridge was going to be tricky to cross, especially at night, with only a reflector belt to show me up. It was a narrow version of two lanes and about 300 meters, or yards, long. Sadly, it was almost completely dark before I reached it. I could almost see there was no walkway, just a foot-wide edge to the parapet. This was going to be tricky. I would need to be on the opposite side of the road from any passing vehicle and if two large trucks were both crossing, I was going to be in squashed trouble.

The railway bridge was 100m upstream but it was too dark now to find a path to it, and I decided to take my chances with the road bridge.

I ran most of the way and only had to dodge across to the other side five times in 300m. so, not much traffic! I reached the island between the two branches of the river, where another 300m bridge awaited. Once across to the other side, I had time to take in the great view of the snowy fields in the moonlight on that still late June evening, take possession of my pack again and wait for my ride to Geraldine to come from farther north. There was no performance that evening and I was delighted to be taken to a warm, inviting, and frankly five-star semi-guest house, where I would stay two nights. Snow lay around and the locals seemed quite used to it.

Day Nineteen—Rangitata to Winchester (sixteen kilometers or ten miles)

Geraldine is the apex of a triangle between two points on the main road, Rangitata and Winchester, and the next day I asked my hostess, Hilary Muir, for a ride back to where I, and my pack, had been picked up, so that I could walk the gap, the hypotenuse, and thus keep up my goal of walking every inch, from the Marlborough Sounds to Bluff.

It was just a short leg of the triangle and I got back to Geraldine soon after lunch and was ready for another performance, a delightful occasion, in a warm small church filled with Bible society members and followers from a wide range of denominations and the Bible Society of New Zealand president from Wellington was there to see what work I was doing in his name.

I began with an introduction of myself in the same way that Maori people define themselves by saying what their mountain, river, and tribe are. Few New Zealanders do not live under the shadow of a mountain, or at least a large hill, and the mountain, river, or lake and tribe are supposed to be consistent, at least from the same district. But in saying that my mountain is Taranaki, my river Whanganui, and my lake Rotorua, I was defining myself, telling much of the tale of my fifty-plus years. And after the performance that evening I turned again to Jesus's journey:

"And he saw them toiling in rowing; for the wind was contrary unto them: and about the fourth watch of the night he cometh unto them, walking upon the sea, and would have passed by them. But when they saw him walking upon the sea, they supposed it had been a spirit, and cried out: For they all saw him, and were troubled. And immediately he talked with them, and saith unto them, Be of good cheer: it is I; be not afraid." Mark 6: 48-50 (KJV)

Jesus's walking on the water is a journey of faith, one that Jesus undertakes after a night spent praying on the side of a mountain while He watches his disciples rowing in a futile battle with the wind. It's a thrilling and uplifting story of what can be achieved through faith. The other gospel accounts have slight variations, with Matthew 14 telling of Peter starting to sink when he tries to walk on water, and John 6 having Jesus not get in the boat at all. But the three gospels are united in Jesus saying, "It is I, be not afraid."

Branscomb's commentary takes a surprising turn here. He says the story can only be a "pious legend" and says there is no basis in other scripture, notably the Old Testament, for Jesus to perform this miracle. The renowned scholar says, "It seems easiest to suppose that there was some incident which furnished the starting point for the legend, but it is idle to conjecture exactly what happened." He says the story of the storm at sea "May have colored the account to some extent".

So, let's put this "pious legend" theory back in the box. It is agreed that Mark, as Peter's follower and interpreter, wrote the gospel following a request from Peter's flock in Rome. Peter would have told Mark about his and Jesus's walking on the water. Peter was the source of Mark's writings. So, Mark hears the story from an eyewitness, certainly a pious tale, but not a legend.

Day Twenty–Winchester to Timaru (twenty-four kilometers or fifteen miles)

The walk next day, to Timaru, was again almost flat. I started from Winchester where my host dropped me off, the point I had walked to the previous day, and now about thirty kilometers (twenty miles) stretched before me.

There was still plenty of snow about to make the country picturesque and the school at Winchester still had children playing outside, waiting for lessons to start, at 9 a.m. as I set off. The first stop was Temuka, about eight kilometers (five miles) down the road.

At one point three huge Clydesdale horses came over to see me. Motorists miss that sort of interaction. Animals, cows, sheep, and even these big guys, loved to come over to their fence as I walked past. They give the passing cars, even bikes, little regard but one solitary walker is something to stop and have a chat with. I was quite used to it but it's worth noting all the same. It was almost rolling country now. I had seen the last of the Canterbury Plains and the long straights of almost boredom that necessitated my games of cricket.

At Temuka the town clock showed 6C (43F) but the locals tell me it is a dry cold. I have heard of a dry heat but not a dry cold! Another little saying coursed through my head and I wrote it down, a quote from Goethe, "Whatever you can do, or dream you can do, begin it. Boldness has genius, power, and magic in it. Begin it now." As the afternoon began, I contacted *The Timaru Herald* and agreed to meet a reporter as I walked into Timaru, which I expected to reach about 3 p.m.

I told them I was ten kilometers (six miles) out of the center but was dismayed to read, another one kilometer closer, that I had twelve kilometers to go. That's not much to a motorist but I was walking every step. From here on to the end of the journey, the inconsistencies in distance measuring increasingly marked.

The reporter reached me and the article she wrote is reprinted in the appendices, and below is the photograph that adorned the front page of the paper the next day. We had a lot of fun obtaining it. She and the photographer drove me to a windy hill above the town, found me a stick, and got me to climb into my costume and wave. The results speak for themselves.

A fine winter day in the hills above Timaru.
Photo courtesy of Stuff Ltd.

That evening a smallish crowd was present, about 30 it seemed, but they probably contributed about $10 each because they gave me a cheque for $145. One or two asked after my father because Dad had finished his working life in Timaru and been a member of a Presbyterian church in the town. I did not tell them he'd quit being a stalwart of the church. One asked me how I was being funded and was surprised that his donation and those of his fellows were enough to keep me going. As I went to sleep that evening, I did a quick tot up; $300 in the first week; $300 in the second week; nearly $600 this week, and an equal amount to the Bible Society in New Zealand. After the performance I again turned to Jesus's story:

> "And Jesus went out, and his disciples, into the towns of Caesarea Philippi: and by the way he asked his disciples, saying unto them, Whom do men say that I am?" Mark 8: 27 (KJV)

Imagine this journey. Jesus and His disciples are walking along in a group. Jesus suddenly stops and waits for his disciples to stop too. Now He has their attention, He poses an important question, to which He knows the answer. Given Peter's prominent role in the subsequent Q&A session, when Peter says, "You are the Messiah!", it must be a tale Peter passes on to Mark, for the gospel writer to record. A careful reading of Mark's gospel finds no instance where Jesus says He is the Messiah, until his interrogation by the Sanhedrin.

In this passage, He tells Peter to say no more about the Messiah and then begins a short, but profound, sermon about what He expects from those who would follow Him. From this point, Jesus regularly calls Himself the "Son of Man", though He has first used the expression in Mark 2, "The Son of Man is Lord also of the Sabbath" (KJV). But from this point on, Jesus uses the term often, when referring to His approaching suffering, death, and return in Glory.

While "Son of Man" can refer to a man born of women, it was also accepted in Biblical times to refer to an apocalyptic figure, an eschatological or "End Times" figure. And it's an indication, says Branscomb, that Jesus accepts the inevitability of His coming death and resurrection.

Day Twenty-One –Timaru to Wainono Turnoff (thirty-eight kilometers or twenty-four miles)

The next morning my kind hosts dropped me off in the middle of town, whence they had plucked me. It was dark when we rose and still dark when I set off, buying the paper, seeing the above, and trudging for about half an hour out of town.

That morning I reflected on the wonderful hospitality so far, but thought little of what lay ahead. Somehow, that was in the Lord's hands and I rejoiced in the warmth and love, as the temperature struggled to stay above freezing and as the sun failed to appear through the strengthening drizzle. I recapped and thought again of the variety of the welcomes I had received. It was now June 27 and I was twenty days into the walk, and had fifteen days to go, all in the Lord's hands.

Easy to put things in God's hands when yours are full, or your feet, because a lot of road lay ahead and I planned to stay in the Waimate camping ground. That was forty-two kilometers (twenty-six miles) away according to the first, hopfully unreliable, road sign, and the rain was thickening. Yikes! But the next road sign contained better news, that Pareora and morning tea/ lunch were just twelve kilometers(eight miles) away.

It was a wet day outside, but I was almost in a state of euphoria, and rang my friend Mike Regan by cell phone to tell him so. I told him that this journey/walk was the most satisfying enterprise of my young life, so far.

I did not use the phone box I found on the road. It was a little piece of history. A red wooden phone box just like the ones with EIIR on them that used to be on every corner. When Telecom took over our lives as well as our communications, they painted them all blue. That was a blue in the sense of the wrong thing to do. The public cried out, at a time when the public thought such cries would make a difference to the multinationals. So, it was a moment of nostalgia when I stepped in and thought about ringing Mike. But then I was jolted back to the 21st century when I found the phone removed. By vandals or Telecom? It made no difference. Where the phone had been was a bit of graffiti, "Teachers are worth more" You can ponder the irony of that for hours. I still am.

And I plugged on into the southerly, dodging trucks' spray and reading crosses. I wondered how an atheist's roadside passing would be marked. A cross may be the symbol of Christ crucified but I am sure the atheist's family would still put one up. Again, the sign distances were inconsistent and confusing. I determined just to keep going as long as it took.

After a quick lunch at St Andrews and the dramatic Celtic High Cross, it was a long haul and more rain until the Makikihi Hotel loomed into view. I paused there for a swift lemonade and told them I was heading for the turnoff to Waimate (where I planned to put my thumb up and return to the main road the next morning). The locals were full of wise words, "It gets late early round here", warning about the sudden arrival of the night on rainy, overcast days in the middle of winter, and a reminder that local quaintness is universal.

I battled on and was still about ten kilometers (six miles) from my destination when another moment that summed up this wonderful part of the world occurred, one I have mentioned in passing at least twice before. The van that stopped was beaten up, to say the least. Its occupants were also worn by many hard-lived years. But their hearts shone and made mine leap when they pulled alongside and asked if I wanted a ride.

"No, thank you, but my pack does."

"We are going to Kurow, via Waimate."

"Fine, can you take the pack to the tearooms at the turnoff? Please tell them I will be there about 5 p.m."

"OK!", and off their red van sped. I figured if they were generous and kind enough to offer me a lift without my asking, they could be trusted with my pack (though I kept my wallet on me).

I knew the town they were heading for and knew they'd be another hour on the road at least and not get home until well after dark.

About 20 minutes later they were back, to say the tearooms, at the turnoff to Route 82, would close before 5 p.m. and the owner was heading for a rugby match further north, in Christchurch. So, they'd come back to tell me the pack was hidden in an old bread delivery bin around the back. And off they went, to catch up with their journey, delayed by a twenty-kilometer round trip. That little piece of kindness has stayed with me for years, until I've come to write it down.

I reached the turnoff, found the pack, and hitched a ride to Waimate, from a local who stopped with a greeting, "You're the walker !" and kindly showed me the camping ground, which had rooms for $10, and the nearby hotel, where I dined and took an early night, as the rain continued to pour down.

Walk in the rain and you'll get to see the rainbow", I thought to myself as I drifted off to sleep.

"And after six days Jesus taketh with him Peter, and James, and John, and leadeth them up into an high mountain apart by themselves: and he was transfigured before them." Mark 9:2 (KJV)

We may find this journey hard to understand, but not hard to visualize, as it is very graphic. Typically, in Mark anyway, Jesus takes His trusty trio of Peter, James, and John. Also typically, Peter, the action man, is quick to react when he sees Jesus talking to Moses and Elijah. He offers to build shelters for all three.

God's message, from the cloud that then covers all six on the mountain, is almost identical to the one at Jesus's Baptism. The first, is Mark 1, "Thou art my beloved Son, in whom I am well pleased". (KJV) This is a message to Jesus alone, while the second, heard on the mountain, is for the disciples, who will carry on Jesus's work, "This is my beloved Son. Hear him." (KJV)

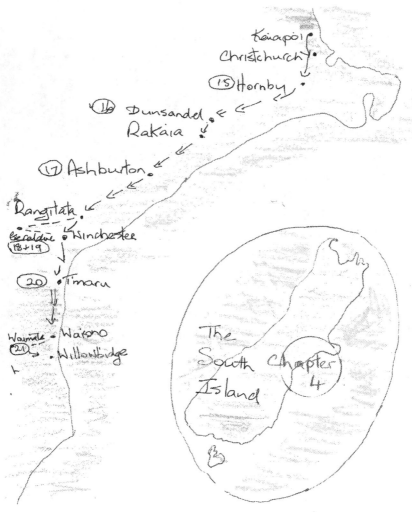

Days fifteen to twenty-one: 215 kilometers (135 miles)

CHAPTER FIVE

Day Twenty-Two–Waimate to Pukeuri (thirty-eight kilometers or twenty-four miles)

FROM WAIMATE, A long day's walking lay ahead. It was mostly flat and from now until my second performance in Dunedin, life and travel (which were very much intertwined) got complicated. Some of it was even backward and I reasoned the complicated first leg thus:

Waimate is one point of an equilateral triangle, with the turn-off where I had stopped last night another point, and Willowbridge, farther south on State Highway 1, the third. I thought I could either hitch a ride back northward, to last night's finishing point (the tearooms), and turn south to walk the main highway, or I could cover the same distance on quieter roads, by taking the Waimate to Willowbridge leg. I chose the latter, to save time waiting for a lift on a day in which I had little time to spare. The map, at the end of the last chapter, shows the triangle, though not accurately to scale. It was fine weather as I left after breakfast at the tearooms. I looked around this quiet little town, walked back to the main road, and paused at the cemetery where former Prime Minister Norman Kirk is buried. Norm or Big Norm, as he was universally known, had died in office after a short illness that took his strength and most of his size away. That was in 1974, just two years after his Labour Party, certainly left of center but no more socialist than any other in New Zealand since 1935, took power from the conservatives, for the first time in twelve years. There were a few conspiracy theories at the time, that he'd been nobbled by the CIA, for example, but such theories do not last long in New Zealand. We are too used to just getting on with it, and so did I.

Boy, it was a long walk, a heavy pack, and a late lunch on the shores of the Waitaki River. I stoked up on anything I could as the memory of the rolling plains behind me receded. Despite the careless dietary regime that I followed on my days on the march, I lost ten kilograms (twenty-two pounds), and tipped the scales close to 90kg (200 lbs.) at the journey's end. Today was not a day to relax too long as I was not sure if I'd see Oamaru before dark.

Just after lunch, the phone rang; it was a proprietor of a luxury bed and breakfast hotel in Oamaru, who had heard the local radio talking about what I was doing and offered me a place to stay the night. That was very kind of him but I had accepted the offer of some Salvation Army people, an always hospitable denomination, and I had to decline. I was not due to present Mark in Oamaru, at the Salvation Army Church Hall, until two days later, for a Sunday evening service.

Thus, I planned to walk on farther south from Oamaru the next day, at the end of which I would get a ride even farther south with the Bible society organizer, Margaret Black. She lived even farther south, in Dunedin. Confused? (See the map at the end of this chapter. But wait, there is more complication ahead.)

As the sun set, "It gets late early around here," I stood at a spot on the 45th parallel, halfway from the South Pole to the Equator, and admired the beauty of the marker cairn as it pierced the sunset behind it. At that moment I surrendered a grudge I had been carrying, forgave a grievance, and found, looking back on that moment, that I could never pick it up again. I can remember it, and know that it happened, but as surely as it happened is the certainty that I have rid myself of the anger associated with it. As I pass the 45 degrees South marker, I may recall the hurt but more importantly recall my act of forgiving, in Jesus's name. And then I will recall all He has forgiven me.

It would be two days before I would stand up and utter the words in the gospel about forgiving when you stand up to pray, if you have any grudge against someone, and then receiving God's forgiveness. At this marker for 45 South, I will always know that I forgave and that my Lord forgives me.

After sunset comes the dark, which I already knew, so with nine kilometers (five and half miles) to go into Oamaru, up went the thumb, soon came the ride which dropped me off near the guest house that had offered me the night's accommodation. I'd said I'd call in if possible and maybe I will again stay there another time. I met my kind would-be hosts, we chatted and I waited for my real host to pick me up and take me right into the small town of Oamaru.

It was a much humbler abode to which I now went. But the home of Keith and Cherie Creighton, on the hill above Oamaru, burst at the seams with love and devotion, not just to Jesus but to every one of His creatures. Missions and other good works abounded and these people welcomed everyone with all their hearts.

They also gave me a ride the next morning, to where my journey had been cut short by nightfall, and waited for me to walk back, pick up my pack from them, and walk past on the road south.

Day Twenty-Three—Pukeuri to Hampden (forty-two kilometers km or twenty-six miles)

My journey that day, June 29, lay south again and I was scheduled to meet Margaret Black late in the afternoon at the coastal town of Hampden. I had much trudging ahead, first to make up the leeway. I was starting to lose count of the times I had done that! There must be a lesson here. The leeway is part of the journey too.

Then, as I walked through Oamaru I found a section of the town dedicated to the memory of a well-known author Janet Frame who was brought up there, attempted misguidedly to be a teacher and, on suffering a breakdown, was committed to a local mental asylum, where her genius was discovered. After narrowly averting a lobotomy, she went to London and wrote of the experience in *Owls Do Cry*. Her dense and utterly satisfying writing came from equally utter and impenetrable shyness but I have the equal satisfaction of being able to say that she's seen me act. And she was impressed enough, not necessarily with me, to break through her shyness and come into the theatre's bar afterward to meet us actors. Someone said, pointing to the pleasant featured late middle-aged woman, "That's Janet Frame". Now it was our turn to be struck with a shyness mixed with awe. That was the root of her shyness, that she was in awe of her talent.

Ahead lay rolling hills and mist rolling into another wet day. I'd left Oamaru at 9 a.m., with nine kilometers (five and half miles) behind me already. Ahead lay another thirty kilometers (twenty miles) all with my pack, and by now I was daily revising Chapter 13. I ran through it more and more easily as the words became familiar, likewise the prompts, and the keys.

The art of learning lines, or anything I suppose, is to give yourself solid keywords and prompts that open the next passage. The mind is just like a computer and opening another "folder" or "cabinet" will allow you to see what is there. All that's needed to go further is to leave another prompt for the next step. That's why verse is so simple to learn. At Herbert, and with ten kilometers (six miles) to go, another Bible society supporter came out to meet me in the grey cold drizzle, take me into her home for afternoon tea, which warmed my heart and inspired my feet, and give me gloves, seeing that I lacked them.

I kept them for a long time, certainly until the end of the walk, and despite my propensity to lose things, had them for long after that, one of them anyway. It was nearly dark again when I reached Hampden and my destination for the day. Some solid rolling hills lay behind and I waited for Margaret who was going to drive me to Palmerston, twenty-five kilometers (fourteen miles) farther south. There lay more warmth at the home of Jan and Bernie where I planned to stay two nights, which became four, with theirs and the Lord's generosity.

Confused? At this point, it might be best to consult the map and think of a game of leapfrog, with Jesus and the Bible society all playing to send me farther south, but not every day. To summarize, on the day I left Oamaru, I walked south to Hampden, where Margaret Black took me farther south to Palmerston, to Jan and Bernie's house in Palmerston.

Day Twenty-Four–Palmerston to Hampden (twenty-five kilometers or sixteen miles)

The next day I walked north from Palmerston back north to Hampden, again in bleak drizzle but without my pack, to wait for Margaret. I went through Chapter 13 again, because I planned to slot that in after Chapter 12 (its proper place) and before I got to Chapter 14. It was always a relief to get to Chapter 14, which I had done so many more times—by itself at Easter for the last few years, for example. At the start of Mark 14, two days before Passover, I knew I had just 20 minutes to go and the action was full on from that point. Unlike the road that stretched before me, which consisted of little traffic and less protection from the weather. By mid-morning, I had reached the sea again, at Shag Point, and saw the Moeraki Boulders on the beach below. At Shag Point, several kilometers south of Moeraki, the boulders looked half-formed, broken even, compared with their perfect brothers and sisters at Moeraki Beach, which lay close to my destination that afternoon.

The scientific explanation is they are five-million-year-old septarian concretions, formed in the seabed of Paleocene mudstone and exposed by coastal erosion. One two-meter (seven ft. diameter boulder is partially embedded in the cliff above the forty or so boulders that sit on the beach and in the shallows. But the native Maori explanation was of large gourds thrown overboard from an equally large mythical canoe. In any event, it is worth an internet search. The Moeraki Boulders are, as the saying goes, "World famous in New Zealand."

Margaret was right on time and we enjoyed the trip back to Oamaru and pleasantly rode over the path I'd walked in the other direction the day before. It was a delight to perform for a good company in Oamaru and raise a decent sum for the Bible society.

I would not have missed the time under the auspices of the Salvation Army in Oamaru for the world. I took one quick look at the plush carpet-lined meeting room and sound-absorbing seats and just as rapidly accepted the offer of a microphone. My voice would have been lost in the well-padded place. We attracted about 200 people which was a considerable proportion of the small town's population. After the performance, Margaret drove me back to Palmerston for the second time in two days.

All very well and hardly complicated, until you remember Margaret was traveling to and from Dunedin, still two days walk away for me. She had first picked me up as she was returning from a cycle race. Margaret and her husband were keen racing cyclists.

After I settled into the warm luxury of the new house in Palmerston and quickly developed an affinity with my hosts, they suggested I use their house as a base for my walk into Dunedin, still fifty kilometers (thirty miles) to the south. Bernie commuted daily to Dunedin and offered his services as a support driver for my walk south. Bernie and Jan also offered a bed for the next two nights.

Day Twenty-Five—Palmerston to Waitati (thirty-five kilometers or twenty-two miles)

I began another day without a pack as I headed out early. The plan, thanks to my hosts' generosity and strategic thinking, was for me to walk south about sixteen kilometers (ten miles) to Waikouaiti, have an early lunch, and then do twenty kilometers (twelve miles) to Waitati. There, Bernie would pick me up at the gas station on his way home from work in Dunedin. The next day he would carry my pack to Dunedin while I completed the Waitati–Dunedin leg and walked on to Margaret Black's home in the center of the city.

In the middle of Palmerston, I stopped at the war memorial. Perusing the large number of names of the fallen, I realized that young men from the district must have volunteered in their droves for the South African Boer War of 1898–1901, and taken their horses so they could be part of the mounted rifles regiments. They were motivated by the call to fight for King and Empire, against the Dutch settlers, the Boers, who wanted to establish an independent state. Such a rallying cry would not generate the same enthusiasm today. My great-grandmother Alice's two younger brothers both served in that way and thankfully were not among the casualties. The numbers for World War I casualties were about the same, but many fewer for World War II.

This was the center of New Zealand's population at that time. The drift north, to a better climate and more opportunities, did not begin until after World War I, and these monuments, depicting a sacrifice that seemed unbearable for such small hamlets, testified to their previous larger size. Nevertheless, those sacrifices were huge.

New Zealand's losses in both world wars were greater than any other nation's, per head of population, and have, I believe, much to do with our present foreign policy, which is not making enemies and relying on the best defense any country could have, the 2,000 kilometers (1200 miles) of Pacific Ocean, Tasman Sea and Southern Ocean, that surrounds New Zealand We take seriously our national anthem, *God Defend New Zealand.*

This was a repositioning day, solid, without-pack walking, and I was enjoying it. The gentle little town of Waikouaiti, another with a war memorial that seemed too big for the town's current size, provided lunch and I knew that the Kilmog, a steep part of the road, was just ahead. I did not linger over lunch. I was right. Soon after lunch, the road curved toward the tough climb that daunted the motorists of yesteryear. They had carried extra water to cool their boiling radiators, before engineers learned how to make the roads more gentle.

I found broad expanses now, the rough edges of the Kilmog smoothed out with large road construction projects over the years, and as rain poured down, I welcomed the fact that I had it easy. I was going to get a ride, backward again, another forward walk the next day and all I had to do was keep walking, something I loved to do. It was a happy time, albeit a little cold.

Day Twenty-Six—Waitati to Dunedin (twenty-five kilometers or sixteen miles)

The next morning, I rode with Bernie to Waitati, the coastal town where he'd picked me up the evening before, and from this point on, all my rides were forward. I could not walk on the main road, as that meant walking on the short stretch of road called the Dunedin Motorway but still a dual carriageway. Instead, I took the Mt. Cargill Road.

After walking through the waking township of Waitati, I started to climb the alternative road that I had driven a few times. I was grateful to have no pack, as I found not only the road was steeply alternative but so were many of the lifestyle blocks I passed. This was the second Waitati of my journey; the first was near my campsite north of Kaikoura. "Wai" is the Maori word for water and water place names are often duplicated; indeed, there are 13 "Wairoa" of various forms throughout the country; rivers, towns, plains, etc.

I admired the dry-stone walls and reflected on how this part of New Zealand was one of its cradles, richly steeped in that great Presbyterian commandment, "Thou Shalt Not," but the product of the great Calvinistic work ethic, nevertheless. I had arranged with *The Otago Daily Times* to meet a reporter at the top, where the road looked down on Dunedin's Port Chalmers, and being a journalist myself, I was impressed with the punctuality of the newspaper's news team and I was also grateful for the article that appeared the next day, accompanied by a picture of me with Port Chalmers in the background, the spot where my great-great-grandfather John Darling and his family disembarked, after a long voyage from Scotland, in January 1858. I walked on, skirting the tops with the port below me until the road started down again and into Dunedin.

I chose the steepest road into the city but it was nowhere near as steep as Baldwin Street, which I passed. This street is officially the steepest in New Zealand and every year the city holds an annual race up, and down. That's just one of the many eccentric things people in Dunedin will do, as the town is dominated by students, or "scarfies", as the locals call them. The street is not long but so steep that few pictures do it justice. I paused below it long enough to learn that I would miss the annual run by just a few days, and I looked up the street long enough to admire the art of a fearless young friend of mine in the North Island who has unicycled down it, no mean feat.

I stopped at Bernie's office to get my pack and arranged to meet him the next day, when I was to be a guest of Dunedin Rotary. Then I walked on to Margaret's house where a warm bath awaited. That evening I presented Mark with a small showing in a modern Salvation Army sanctuary setting. I was advised to use a mike but did my usual boast about my big voice. Very soon I realized that even those people four rows back could not hear me and decided to pick up the microphone. The acoustics were so dead because the building had previously been a nightclub, with fully baffled walls and a thick carpet that completed the process. That evening, snug at Margaret Black's home, I thought again of Jesus's journey.

> "And they departed thence, and passed through Galilee; and he would not that any man should know it. For he taught his disciples, and said unto them, The Son of Man is delivered into the hands of men, and they shall kill him; and after that he is killed, he shall rise the third day." Mark 9: 30-31 (KJV)

This is more than just a journey through Galilee and toward Jerusalem. It's one of Jesus' journeys away from the public and it's the second of Jesus's attempts to tell the disciples what lies in store for them. Jesus first briefly alludes to His fate when descending the "Transfiguration" mountain.

It's a journey of explanation and repetition. They say that just when you are 'blue in the face" from constantly telling something, from repeating yourself time and again, your audience is hearing the message for the first time. And so it is with Jesus. In Mark 10:32, Jesus again explains what lies ahead for Him. This time He has more detail and gives more hope when He says that on the third day He shall rise to life. It's doubtful the disciples get the message at this, the third time of hearing. They need to hear it again before the other shoe drops.

Day Twenty-Seven—Dunedin to East Taeri (fifteen kilometers or nine miles)

We began the next day with a dawn service in the Anglican Cathedral in the Octagon. Most cities have a square but Dunedin has an Octagon, with a statue of Robbie Burns. He sits with his back to the church and faces the public house on the other side of the square.

At the service, taken by Margaret in the small side chapel, I met several who had been on the Hikoi of Hope five years before. A hikoi is a New Zealand tradition. The Maori word means a communal walk or march for publicity or protest. The most well-known was the 1977 land march which embraced Maori people, mostly, who walked from both ends of New Zealand to meet in Wellington and highlight the real grievances of Maori land rights advocates. Some decided to camp on Parliament grounds when it was over and formed a tent city that both embarrassed the establishment and highlighted their cause.

Margaret has also arranged an interview for me with local television, which boosted my second performance, and I spent the rest of the day walking farther south, minus pack, to the suburban extremities of Dunedin. I got a bus back. It was a dull grey mid-winter day but I enjoyed the fifteen kilometers I made to the southern outskirts, to where Margaret drove me the next morning.

The evening performance was at the South Dunedin Presbyterian church, a place my grandfather had taught Sunday School in, 100 years before. I treasure a photograph taken in 1903 of the Sunday School teachers there. Fred Darling was a devout man and would have been a Presbyterian minister if a "weak chest" had not dissuaded him. Instead, he became a builder, lived a long and productive life, and died at 90, with his weak chest improved by an active life.

The church's wooden pews, floor, walls, and ceiling made my voice sing and the acoustics were a joy to use. I did not need a microphone, It was a much larger gathering as well, all absorbing the elements of Jesus's journey.

> "And when he was gone forth into the way, there came one running, and kneeled to him, and asked him, Good Master, what shall I do that I may inherit eternal life?" Mark 10: 17 (KJV)

> Jesus may be on a journey, but the man who accosts Him has a greater journey, He must go from his confident repetition of the Ten Commandments and his assurance that he's kept them since a boy, to the slow realization of what Jesus asks him to do, because selling his property and giving the money to the poor is quite beyond his capacity for self-sacrifice. Jesus continues the man's journey as He explains that it is very hard for rich people to get into God's Kingdom, something that dismays the disciples, who ask how anyone can get into the Kingdom.

> Jesus's answer is oblique but satisfactory, saying some things people cannot do, but God can do anything. Which we can take to mean that we should not worry and just have faith. However, Peter continues to protest,

pointing to the sacrifices he and the other disciples made and Jesus gives them the tough message, that their journey will bring rewards on one hand and mistreatment on the other, but in the world to come, eternal life. The disciples accept the rewards, and drawbacks, and carry on. But the man who cannot give up his possessions is left to return to them. And wonder, as he examines them, what might have been?

Day Twenty-Eight–East Taeri to Waihola (twenty-four kilometers or fifteen miles)

Now my thoughts turned even more ancestrally, to my grandfather Fred's grandfather, John Darling, and to John's son James. I only had a short distance to walk that day, then another day's walk to Milton and a third to Balclutha. According to the account of John Darling's "hikoi", with his family from Dunedin to Balclutha, their journey took three and a half days, the same as it took me. And they began late because the dray to take women and small children was late.

To begin at the beginning, I am delighted to include, in the appendix, the complete record from the book about their settlement, written in 1958 by Mrs. Alma Rutherford, and reprinted here with the kind permission of the author's family.

John and Janet Darling arrived from Edinburgh with their small brood, including great-grandpa James, in Dunedin in early 1858. He had just turned 10. The family had decided to emigrate because Janet (nee Park) wanted to start a fresh life. John's first wife, my great-great-grandmother, had died in childbirth in 1848 but the baby James survived. John remarried and began another family, despite having several adult children, all of whom he farewelled forever at Edinburgh when the *Strathallen* sailed in the northern summer of 1857. They teamed up with another Edinburgh family, the Smaills, and between them were a total of four men, four women, and ten children. The youngest Smaill had been born just a month before.

Curiously, their journey to Balclutha mirrored mine, despite the gap of 150 years. On the first day, they only got as far as I had on my second day in Dunedin (when I caught the bus back). Their household effects had been sent around the coast by steamer and Andrew Smaill also went ahead with his oldest son to prepare a meal on their arrival.

That first day the men and older children walked either in front or behind the dray. Like them, my day began early. By midday, I was at the spot they also reached at midday on the second day, the Taieri River. They traveled on the waterway to make more rapid progress than I, walking along the riverbank on a road that did not exist in early March (late summer) 1858, and along the great straights of the Taieri Plains.

They stopped for the night to camp near Lake Waihola, while I had accommodation and a meal arranged, at the same lake. I dined with people who were keen to feed me in Jesus's name and then stayed the night with a gentleman with whom I discoursed long into the night, about Jesus of course.

As I walked, I rang a friend by cell phone to tell him I had a story and picture published in the *Otago Daily Times*. My friend then found it on his computer. He downloaded both the picture and story and I wondered about the strange conversation my forebears might have had about it. Imagine my great-great grandfather John Darling telling his ten-year-old son, "James, one day, 150 years in the future, your great-grandson will walk beside this river. It will be a huge road by then, with incredible conveyances traveling faster than any speeding locomotive, and he'll call a friend 1,000 miles away on his cell phone. His friend will download the newspaper, story, and picture, with a computer via the internet."

Little of that would have made sense to young James Darling. Unimaginable? Of course, just as the next 150 years are unimaginable to us.

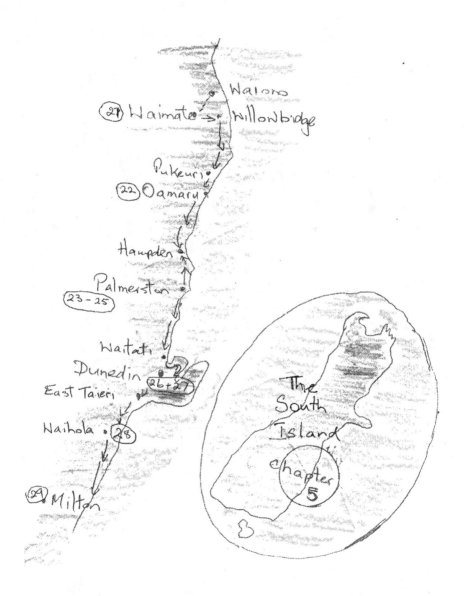

Days twenty-two to twenty-eight: 204 kilometers (130 miles)

CHAPTER SIX

Day Twenty-Nine–Waihola to Milton
(fifteen kilometers or nine miles)

THE NEXT MORNING, I walked beside the same lake my forebears had sailed along. On this still and misty morning, I could not help thinking how proud they would be of the improvements their descendants had made to the land and the lake. It was quite unlike the lake they had found but nature still dominated. Although the dense native forest had become pristine pasture, nature was still in charge. Mist and a biting wind were enough natural elements to be going on with.

A car stopped and gave me some welcome sustenance, a couple of biscuits and a drink. A friend in the North Island had asked them to watch out for me. The pair were on their way to the Catlins, on the southeast coast, and I promised to visit them on my way back.

Then I turned my face south and headed for Milton and another performance. I reached it late on my second day from Dunedin, the same spot the Darling/Smaill party had reached, although they called it Tokomairiro then. Milton was a joy. I arrived in the mid-afternoon and had time to meet my hosts, a young family who had cleared out the guest room for me. The local bible society was stronger than many in much larger towns. This little town had a great turnout, easily 100, in the Presbyterian Church Hall. It was not in the church itself. That stayed closed in the winter months due to heating costs. The congregation was too small now to warrant the expense and the hall was much cozier.

I sat them in a horseshoe of chairs and they were about three or four deep. This attentive audience comprised dedicated souls. Some of them were very young, one or two too young to concentrate, or even stop crying. The young (crying) family sat in the front row and I kept thinking of Jesus' lines about little children belonging in God's Kingdom, and how it was only possible to get into God's Kingdom by seeing it the way they did. The earnest faces of their parents left me in no doubt they wanted their children to hear the message and I was thrilled to deliver it. This crowd was alive, taking the time to come out on a cold winter night and we were all rewarded by it. Milton might have been small but it was a tremendously embracing place to present the gospel. Afterward, the couple who had brought their five children, it could have been more, noted that I had played seven different characters in one passage. They were counting! It was my great reward for perseverance and understanding because several times I had wanted to ask them to take the children out. Jesus gently stopped me and I found my reward later.

> "And when they came nigh to Jerusalem, unto Bethphage and Bethany, at the mount of Olives, he sendeth forth two of his disciples. And saith unto them, Go your way into the village over against you: and as soon as ye be entered into it, ye shall find a colt tied, whereon never man sat; loose him, and bring him."
> Mark 11:1-2 (KJV)

And so begins the journey into Jerusalem, and so begins Palm Sunday. Mark's Gospel does not mention that Jesus had been in Jerusalem before, though His visits are marked four times in John. Jesus had probably been to Jerusalem, although it was a three-day walk from His home district of Galilee. His reception was certainly not the parade of an unknown but of an eagerly awaited celebrity, whom the people of Jerusalem had talked about often. As early as Mark 3, we learn how large crowds came out from Jerusalem, and as far as Tyre and Sidon because they heard what Jesus was doing. Now they had a chance to welcome Him into their home, just as we have the daily delight of welcoming Him

93

in our hearts. Scholars, like Branscom, eschew that spiritual angle but start to quibble about the geography Mark mentions, wondering why, as a Jerusalem native, Mark, was not more accurate. Such academic over-thinking often buries the faith message, the "Alleluia" and "Hosanna" of Palm Sunday.

Branscom says Mark understands it to be the entrance, into Jerusalem, of Zion's King and indeed, from this moment there is a change in Jesus's message. He is no longer hiding the fact he is the Christ, the Messiah, and is building toward His interrogation by the High Priest of the Temple when He declares directly that He is the Christ.

Day Thirty–Milton to Balclutha (twenty-five kilometers or sixteen miles)

The reward and memory of that satisfying night's work stayed with me as I walked out of Milton and headed for Balclutha. It was another cold and grey day and a borrowed beanie kept me warm. I soon passed the turnoff to the inland road to Lawrence and Gabriel's Gully, which my ancestor John Darling would have taken when he left the farm, for a little while, to seek the gold that had been discovered there, about 50 miles inland. This was the beginning of the 1861 Otago Gold Rush, which put the province on the map and made Dunedin more prosperous than any other New Zealand city, even Auckland.

John would have been about the same age as I, and like me, still optimistic and adventurous in his early fifties. He left behind his son, my great-grandfather James, who was old enough, at thirteen, to handle the farm This was the mid-19th century after all. Back in Britain, lads younger than James were working in apprenticeships, underground mines, and sweatshops of all sizes. Ironically, John Darling had left all that behind, to give his family a better future. I suppose he was seeking gold for the same reason.

Although my forebears on the march had nothing ahead of them until nightfall, I had the luxury of a restored former gracious dwelling for lunch. This was Garvan and its welcome offer of Devonshire tea, with scones, jam, and cream, became a sort of early lunch, as I knew nothing else lay ahead.

In the middle of the afternoon, I was delighted to see Kaitangata in the distance, and rang my friend, the bright sparky Larry Rogers in Taumarunui. He'd once called himself the Kaitangata Kid, being an apprentice electrician in the coal mine. Larry saw the light, as it were, in the middle of the coal mine and went to college, majored in Russian, became an actor, and trod the boards with me about twenty-five years before. He piled a lot more into his rich life than he would have done in staying in the mining town. We often talked of how our forebears might have knocked around together in Kaitangata in the late 1800s, his grandfather and James Darling.

His grandfather, then a young single man, was famously absent from the mine on the day of the 1879 disaster when thirty-four of the forty-seven miners employed at the pit were killed. Larry's ancestor was too tired, hungover, or just plain cussed to go to work that day. Larry painted a picture of men swinging along the road in the early morning, pre-shift dawn. They called out for "Neesy" to show a leg and not be "breezy." Neesy declined to join them, and most of his friends perished. Neesy spent the rest of his life living with that loss, as did the many bereaved women of the town.

A family legend that originated at that time, which I heard from my father, was of James Darling going off to town, to a stock sale for example, with the horse and gig and getting so drunk that he would sleep on the way home. The horse drove him home in the horse's own good time. His wife Alice, both the daughter and grand-daughter of Church of Ireland rectors, and born Alice Cassidy in County Donegal, was so irate at this behavior that she signed the pledge to abstain from alcohol and asked her eight-year-old son Fred, my grandfather, to do the same. Fred never touched a drop, because of that early promise. And I made sure I never took a drink in his presence.

It was about 4 p.m. and getting gloomy when I walked into the Balclutha vicarage, the Anglican minister Graham Langley's house. We'd talked a bit before about my ancestral connection with the town and how the Darlings had farmed a few miles downstream. I met the charming

Mrs. Hannaby, who lived in Clinton, the next town southwest. She was a member of the congregation and was heading thirty kilometers (twenty miles) west to get home before dark. She offered to billet me with her family when I came the next day, although I had no performance planned there. Then the minister drove me for a quick look at Inch Clutha, the river delta island which my ancestors had farmed.

We drove through settled and fenced farmland that looked productive and prosperous and past the stopbanks (levees) that kept the mighty Clutha River at bay. The river is the largest in New Zealand, by water volume, but not the longest. That's the Waikato in the North Island. But the Clutha drains three mighty glacier-formed lakes, themselves fed by the mountain rivers off the great Southern Alps and can flood quite mightily in its turn. The great flood of 1878 was a big setback for my family and there have been many such floods since to compare it with, but none worse.

We did not drive as far as the old Darling homestead at Kemra Bank but visited people who lived, surrounded on four sides by eight-foot-high stopbanks, in a house that matched the age of my great-great-grandfather's. It was quite a moment, to receive the hospitality of people, in this case Mike Horder, a Balclutha lawyer, and his family, whose antecedents had rubbed shoulders with mine. So, when it was offered, I accepted a small glass, a "wee dram", of whiskey although it was just past 5 p.m. and I was due to present Mark in an hour.

One glass may not seem much but it left a little light-headedness that stayed with me for about fifteen minutes of the performance, I regret to admit. One nip glass is a tiny bit of alcohol, but the adrenalin that pumps makes the effects a little noticeable, to the imbiber. I am certain none of the fifty or so who gathered to hear the Word of the Lord would have noticed anything amiss. I am sure there was none actually, but I was just a little concerned. I will say in my defense, that it was a very special glass of Scotch that coursed through my veins, drunk to commemorate the beginnings of my family's life in New Zealand and in no way affecting my memory or the spirit of the occasion. I'm not sure what my grandfather Fred would have said, though.

Once again, I arranged the seating in a horseshoe. I had told the vicar the story of performing to several prisoners and hearing them all whisper "Yes" when I told of Jesus coming to call sinners. So, he was waiting for his flock to utter the same cry of affirmation. He wasn't holding his breath though. He knew his people believed themselves to be good honest folk, who would be piously aghast to know the man dressed in monk's robes in front of them had taken a tipple an hour before, even if it was to honor some honorable men, who also knew Jesus and His journey well.

> "And he sendeth forth two of his disciples, and saith unto them, Go ye into the city, and there shall meet you a man bearing a pitcher of water: follow him". Mark 14: 13 (KJV)

This time the disciples journey into Jerusalem, showing that Jesus and His entourage stayed out of the city, in Bethany, for the duration of His ministry in Jerusalem. A practical interpretation of Jesus's instructions, to find a man who would lead them to a room ready for the Passover meal preparation, etc., is that Jesus may have seen exactly this on a previous walk through Jerusalem; or that such water-carrying men were common in the Holy City.

But let's not overthink it, again. It's a story about Jesus's foresight, which He has hinted at many times when telling the disciples what will happen to Him. As His time of trial draws near, Jesus's journey takes a practical but necessary turn. There are preparations for a meal celebrating not only the Passover but the passing on of His mission, in the form of the Last Supper, of which Mark's gospel makes a simple and direct account.

Day Thirty-One—Balclutha to Clinton (thirty-two kilometers or twenty miles)

The next morning, the Rev. Graham took my pack to Clinton ahead of me and I had the pleasure of a pack-free walk. It was pleasant, rolling country, Northern Southland they called it, and being a stranger, I was struck by the incongruity of such a name. Northern Southland? That's a bit like Southern Northland but at the other end of the country, or Eastern Westland. But I am sure the locals are long used to the incongruity and give it little thought. It was a fine day, uninterrupted by much traffic, and about lunchtime I met the Rev. Graham coming back from dropping my pack off, telling me they were waiting for me excitedly at the other end.

The meeting was a joy and a memory that stays with me always. Twin boys, aged nine, greeted me at the end of my day's walk. They had been waiting since just after lunch, much like I used to wait for the arrival of my grandparents, hour after hour staring into the distance for a green Morris 8 to come round the corner. But these boys were older, and quite shy when they approached me with their first question, "Are you a Christian?"

"Yes"

Whew, they were relieved to find they weren't accosting strangers after all.

"Well, come with us," they said delightedly.

They took me home and I met their two older brothers, four boys in three years must have been a handful but their parents knew they were their greatest blessing. There was no performance of Mark set down in the small town but there was a very interesting impromptu one in their home after dinner.

The four boys normally squeezed into two bedrooms but for my visit, they had put all of them in one room, which created both space for me and an opportunity for mayhem for the lads. Pillow fights erupted long after bedtime and it struck me how rarely this happens in the 21st century, with small families and larger houses.

The boys were charmed by the idea of a "Man of God" walking the length of the South Island and it was mutual because I was, in turn, charmed by such simple and heartfelt Christian beliefs. One boy wanted to buy me something and asked if he could get a packet of biscuits from the local store. It was more than a 10-year-old's desire to get something for himself. It was a genuine desire to give. He got his wish to buy the treat, for someone else.

Day Thirty-Two—Clinton to Gore (forty two kilometers or twenty six miles)

The next morning one of the boys, Corbin, wanted to walk with me a little way out of town. His twin brother also sought an invitation. Then, all said they were going. Their mother thought I might find four of them walking out of town, in the middle of a Southland pre-dawn frost, a bit much to handle so she came along too. I am glad she did. As we walked out of the small town she waved to neighbors, who looked bemused at this strange early-morning parade, and for the next three kilometers (two miles) kept up a constant stream of instruction to the boys who insisted on either walking in the ditch or too far onto the road.

"Corbin, get out of the ditch, Benson get off the road, get out of the ditch, get off the road." They would have walked to Gore with me, all day, but after three kilometers I realized whatever distance we traversed, they would have to repeat. I called for a rest and we bade farewell. By now the boys were hungry, the four boys had missed breakfast, and thankfully there was a packet of biscuits to share. What goes round coming round. And as we prayed for our journeys, theirs and mine, our thoughts turned to the journey of Our Lord.

> "And he went forward a little, and fell on the ground, and prayed that, if it were possible, the hour might pass from him." Mark 14:33 (KJV)

> Jesus knows His last journey is at hand and for the first time in Mark's, or any gospel, we see Him asking for his burden to be taken from Him. This drama comes fully alive in any staged version, certainly in mine, and it must shock anyone hearing, or reading, the story for the first time. They see Jesus, who has confidently predicted His coming death and Resurrection, now asking for a last-minute reprieve. It's for good reason this moment is called the Agony at Gethsemane.

> Before and after Jesus's plea for God to reconsider, He is complete composure, assuring His disciples that all will

be well, and dealing quietly and calmly, even stoically, with His accusers, Pontius Pilate and the High Priest. But not at this moment. So how does Mark the writer know, if not from Peter or other disciples overhearing? We are indebted to Mark and the other gospel writers for bringing Jesus' agony to our notice.

The disciples would have heard Jesus, by now some distance away, bargaining with God. That should have been enough to keep them awake. Without this opening part of Jesus's prayer, the submission to God's will in the second would lack contrast and impact. On hearing Jesus's submission, we know He is prepared to do His Father's bidding, regardless of the cost to Him. And we can take solace and inspiration from His sacrifice at any difficult time in our lives.

Dubbed the Presidential Highway, United States' President Bill Clinton could not resist a chuckle when shown this picture on his 1999 state visit to New Zealand.

Indeed, I was walking from Clinton to Gore, two towns that have been part of New Zealand history long before President Bill Clinton and his running mate, Al Gore, were part of the world scene. In deference to them both, the road I now walked was renamed "The Presidential Highway" and Bill Clinton was very amused to see it on his only visit, so far, to the South Island.

In Gore, I could almost smell my destination, three days away, and I prepared for my performance of Mark, without a microphone, I insisted. I also suggested, as gently but firmly as possible, that everyone should sit up the front. How often do people sit at the back of a sanctuary? I don't like it myself. What is so wrong with the front row, the one that is never filled?

People like to have a pew in front of them but some like to have the whole church, as if they are apologizing for being there. That said, the congregation at Gore was dutiful in sitting up front, except for one middle-aged woman who stayed right at the back.

It was not the best acoustics; they were good enough but plenty of padding deadened them for a voice to be easily heard at the back of the room, so this woman was not hearing me very well. She decided to walk back to the sound box and, imagining I was miked, turned me up. The effect was a lot of feedback and some disconcerting whistles, but my voice did not appear in the speakers because it had not been sent there in the first place.

I was tempted to stop and ask her to come and sit with the others, rather than disrupt things with this display but I'm glad I didn't. They told me later that she still suffered the effects of being locked in cupboards as a childhood punishment, and could not bear to be with, or among, any crowds or congregations. She always sat at the back. In musing over the time spent in the Gore church, and the lesson the woman at the back provided, I turned again to Jesus's journey, now becoming very sad, in contrast to the completion I was starting to feel.

> "And straightway in the morning the chief priests held
> a consultation with the elders and scribes and the whole
> council, and bound Jesus, and carried him away, and
> delivered him to Pilate." Mark 15: 1 (KJV)

Jesus's journey now sees him appear before the Roman authority, the Governor of Judea, Pontius Pilate. It was the next morning, after his trial by the Sanhedrin the night before. Justice was swifter than now, but this is very rapid indeed, and the Jewish leaders may have prepared the trial ahead of time before Jesus was arrested. It's generally accepted that the Roman authorities now controlled the right to impose capital punishment, hence the need to take Jesus to Pilate, on the morning before Passover, which we know as Good Friday.

While the chief priests accused Jesus of claiming to be The Messiah, Pilate interpreted that to mean He was claiming to be the King of the Jews and sought clarification from Jesus, "Thou sayest it," (KJV) says Jesus, which is ambiguous and has been interpreted to mean, "You said so, not me" or to mean the opposite "Certainly." For Pilate, it's enough of an admission for him to put a sign on Jesus's cross, "The King of the Jews".

And so the trial by Pilate takes Jesus on His journey towards death on the cross. While Pilate finds no fault with Jesus (he must not consider a claim to be The Messiah as very serious), he is now facing an angry mob, stirred up by the high priests. He asks what he should do with Jesus and they reply, "Crucify Him!"

Day Thirty-Three—Gore to Wyndham (thirty-one kilometers or nineteen miles)

The next three days passed quickly and, my thoughts on the final goal then drove me rapidly forward. I left my hosts in Gore with a little saying that I'd had from childhood, a morning prayer if you like:

The light of the sun makes bright the day.
After darkest night.
And Oh, my soul, gives thanks to the sun,

For in it shines the light of God,
And Oh, my soul, be up and doing!

And I walked on in a bleak midwinter day, ever further south, to Wyndham where I stayed in a modest motel, warm against the increasing blast. I had an early night as I prepared to battle more dirty weather, forecast the next day, with contemplation of Jesus's now desperate journey.

"And they bring him unto the place Golgotha, which is, being interpreted, The place of a skull. And they gave him to drink wine mingled with myrrh: but he received it not." Mark 15: 22-23 (KJV)

Jesus' journey is nearly over and His mission to bring peace on earth is about to begin. Mark implies that the soldiers gave Jesus the drink as a mercy, but Branscom's research into rabbinical writings shows it was the custom of Jewish women of the city to make this drink and send it to condemned men. In relating Jesus's refusal to drink, Mark emphasizes that He wants to keep alert until the end; alert enough to give advice and encouragement to the two robbers, nailed to crosses beside him, and alert enough to cry out to God in a loud voice, "My God, My God, why have You forsaken Me?

There's a contrast between the drinks. The first, Jesus refuses and then He presumably drinks the second, when offered in the form of a sponge dipped in wine or vinegar or sour wine (depending on the translation), when, according to Mark, a man suggests they wait for Elijah to come to save Jesus.

An opiate drink or a drink in a sponge ? Both give an inferior benefit to the "Cup of Living Water" that Jesus promises us.

Day Thirty-Four—Wyndham to Invercargill (forty-three kilometers or twenty-seven miles)

My day walking into Invercargill was a slog through rain and a picture taken by the local newspaper neatly captured my tiredness that evening. Not that it showed, in a well-attended performance of Mark in Invercargill, in a deeply raked lecture theatre. I stayed two nights in Invercargill, one after walking from Wyndham and another after walking to Bluff and getting a ride back.

My hosts were delightful and suggested that course of action. Like everyone, they were keen to know what I was going to do next, and on the last day, I prayed for guidance on that subject.

One option was to go back and write the trip up while staying in the Peel Forest, another was to cross the strait to Stewart Island and present Mark there. My journey was nearing an end, though Jesus's is ongoing,

> "And when the sabbath was past, Mary Magdalene, and Mary the mother of James, and Salome, had bought sweet spices, that they might come and anoint him. And very early in the morning the first day of the week, they came unto the sepulchre at the rising of the sun. ³And they said among themselves, Who shall roll us away the stone from the door of the sepulchre?" Mark 16: 1-3 (KJV)

This is now the women's journey, of discovery and realization. They think they are walking to Jesus's tomb, expecting to perform their traditional burial rites, washing and anointing the body. Their biggest worry is how to roll the stone away, but that's soon replaced with a bigger worry: How can they tell the others what they have seen? The empty tomb, the young man dressed in white, the instructions to tell the disciples that Jesus will meet them in Galilee. No wonder they run away in fear. Their world has been turned upside down.

This chapter is the center of Christian teaching, explaining that Christians worship the risen Jesus Christ, that His story does not end on the cross and His life transforms from tragedy to triumph.

But Mark's original gospel ends with the women running from the tomb, too afraid to tell anyone. The rest of the story, of Jesus appearing to his 11 disciples and giving instructions for their ministry, was added later. Bible scholars have many theories about the abrupt and questionable end. Some conjectured the last verses were lost before Mark's original manuscript could be copied. Others suggest it was deliberately suppressed because it differed from the other gospel, or that Mark had to leave Rome suddenly. Whatever the reason, the additions make a satisfactory conclusion to Jesus's story.

At one performance I deliberately stopped where Mark stopped and acted as though I'd finished. The audience's looks were astounding. They seemed to say, "Yes, go on."" Why have you stopped? "No, that's not the end," "What's happening?" I explained that was the original Mark ending, and gave them the rest of the chapter, as they knew it. And I resolved never to do that again.

Day Thirty-Five–Invercargill to Bluff (twenty-five kilometers or sixteen miles)

As I walked, without my pack, having left that with my host who would take me from Bluff back to Invercargill, I thought and prayed for clarity to decide what to do next.

An athletic man, a racewalker, had told me after the performance in Invercargill he'd catch up with me on the road. I saw him coming out of the corner of my eye and thought he was running; he was walking so rapidly. He had the grace to slow to my pace and we talked for a while, and then he zoomed away again, leaving me amazed at his speed.

Then my cell phone rang, a theatrical agent wanted me to come back to Auckland for two weeks' work as an extra in a TV shoot. That was the answer to my direct prayer, I thought. I wondered at the parting question, "Do you still have that long grey beard?" I had a trimmed grey beard but, well, length, is a matter of degree, right?

So that was it. I had the answer to my prayer and decided I had to get back to the North Island as soon as possible. I decided to buy a rough, cheap, old car so I could visit the Catlins on the way, and drive back, as quickly as I could.

Two days later, when making my way up the South Island, I got a cancellation call from that same agency. They had made a mistake and I was not the person they wanted. I wondered if sometimes our prayers get intercepted, by the other side. Is that possible?

As I approached Bluff, my host for the final two nights in Invercargill joined me for the last seven kilometers (four miles). Together we reached the famous signpost that points from Bluff to all sorts of places, from Sydney to London, to the South Pole to Los Angeles, etc. And in the shadow of the signpost, all making suggestions for the future, I paused again for a look at Jesus's command.

"And he said unto them, Go ye into all the world, and preach the gospel to every creature." Mark 16: 15 (KJV)

Now the journey is for all of us, beginning with the disciples who spread the Word. Jesus makes it clear that belief and baptism are necessary for salvation, and He promises marvelous powers for those who believe. The most wonderful of these is the ability to lay hands on the sick and heal them. The Acts of the Apostles is full of such examples. For me, reaching this passage is a signal that I'm nearly finished, But, like everything else in our journey with Jesus, as soon as one thing finishes, another starts.

Days twenty-nine to thirty-five: 223 kilometers (133 miles)

CHAPTER SEVEN

MY SOUTH ISLAND walk was a huge step in my life. It was easily the most exciting and worthwhile thing I had done in it, but at age fifty-four, I was sure there was more to come if I left the next step in The Lord's hands. I returned to my brother's flat in Auckland.

Newspaper journalism did not seem to be in my future. While I still had plenty to offer, I could not lose the feeling that the door was shut to me. I tried canvassing for Greenpeace, accosting passers-by on the street with an invitation to join the environmental activists' group. I did not enjoy it, though I felt committed to the cause. I got a few laughs in the almost three weeks I stuck it out. One man called out, as he passed me and the other canvasser, "Oh leave the earth alone you guys." We both saw the funny side. But I soon accepted there is a widespread reluctance to be stopped on the street, no matter how important the cause.

The Bible Society in New Zealand asked me to record my performance and that gave me several light moments, on reflection. The local organizer, Mel Bowen, had already tried getting a live filming, at Mt Maunganui, one of my pre-walk venues, but it was not satisfactory in quality and painfully (for me) recorded a couple of stumbles. So, we arranged another recording and found a venue in Katikati, near Tauranga, and a videographer. A church member followed the CEV version to make sure I was accurate, as the society had asked. They said they wanted the gospel according to St. Mark, not according to Geoffrey. I let that quip go and began.

I got about two minutes into Mark 1 before the prompter called, "Halt!" and pointed out my mistake, words swapped in error. I checked the passage and we began again, starting the tape from where I'd left off, the tape to be edited later. Thus we staggered through three chapters in about three hours. This was obviously not working.

The patient prompter offered to prepare cue cards for me, in large print, of the whole book of Mark. She'd need a week, so we adjourned. On resuming, I found she'd photocopied huge tracts onto large cards for me to read when I felt I needed to.

I have since used a proper teleprompter, but this was our ad hoc version, and it worked. I am blessed with keen distance vision that has remained with me to this day and the cue card experiment worked. The Bible society produced the video and we made no formal agreement about payment, beyond offering to send me a copy.

I thought no more about it, so I was thrilled and amused to hear, ten years later via the now-invented Facebook, from an actor friend who had bought a copy of the VHS recording, at a school rummage sale. She paid $NZ1, which doesn't sound much, about $US0.60c. I resurrected my VHS copy, had it professionally transferred to DVD, and watched it for the first time. I had more light moments as I watched myself. It was hard to tell that I was reading almost everything that came out of my mouth, thanks to the hard work of the woman who prepared all those cue cards, and my 20:10 vision.

Back in Auckland, I took on work as a city bus driver, inspired by the experiences of actors I knew who'd got behind the big wheel between acting engagements. I brought the people into the city in the morning, took a midday break of 3-4 hours, and returned them to their homes in the evening. I liked it and some of the more amusing moments would fill a small book.

Here's just one, and keep in mind Auckland was, and still is, full of young Chinese and South Korean men and women learning English as a second language. On board on this day was a young woman who had just started her studies. These students rarely asked me for a fare to their stop. They'd just get on, without a word, and shove a pre-paid card into the ticket dispenser. I'd been told the Mandarin Chinese words for "Hello" and used them incorrectly to someone who must have been Korean. The scornful hard stare that came back kept me from trying again.

This student, whom I assumed was new, was still on board when we reached the end of the route. She'd either missed her stop or was on the wrong bus. She just shrugged and looked sad and lost. I asked in a quiet, slow, decipherable, voice if she knew her home address. She knew enough to tell me in English. It was about ten minutes away and on a different route. I was supposed to drive to the depot and finish for the day, but I couldn't see any harm in a little detour in a familiar part of Auckland, and I was only ten minutes late back.

I mounted some small tours of St. Mark for the Bible society on the regular four-day weekends our rosters gave us. I used the breaks to tour the North Island's east coast, more than seven hours drive from Auckland, taking in Gisborne and Havelock North, where I got a crowd of at least 300, and my father in the front row, well into his eighties and fast asleep. He was listening with his eyes shut. as he explained to me later. Two other long weekends got me to Palmerston North, Whanganui, Hawera, and New Plymouth.

I had now performed St Mark's Gospel in every New Zealand city with a population of more than 20,000, with one exception, the cathedral city of Nelson at the top of the South Island. At the time of writing that omission has yet to be addressed and I pray I live long enough to go there. So life was settled and revolving around bus driving, St. Mark, and a companionable time with my younger brother Richard, who accepted my staying with the same easy-going nature he'd had all his life.

Rose

But all that changed on December 20, 2003, when I got an email from what I thought was New York, someone called Time2Sing. I'd put myself on an American "dating" program called Christian Singles because I wanted to find someone to help organize a tour of the United States and freshen the sour taste I had about the failure of my walk last time. Christian Singles has since been taken over by something else and has another name, as did someone called Time2Sing.

The first message was short enough to stay in my mind forever. "I know someone who performs Mark's Gospel." I replied, "Oh really, tell me more." We have preserved a hard copy of all the interactions of those first days and look back on them occasionally, especially on December 20, 2023, when we celebrated twenty years since our lives changed forever.

By my third email, I was asking what she was doing still up, because I thought it was midnight in America, not yet as familiar with the time difference as I have become. I sent about 300 words on my first introduction to this book, about performing at a prison farm and the prisoners saying "Yes" when I told them how Jesus said He'd come to call sinners to follow him. We covered a lot in those first days and began warming into a tenderness that surprised and delighted us. At this stage we never expected to meet so we hid nothing from each other Within a few email exchanges, she said she lived just south of Cleveland and her name was Rose, though she'd used Julia Rose Edwards as a pen name. She found it wise to use the anonymity of New York before she got to know someone. We had our eyes wide open and I brewed up a poem to explain my thoughts on internet connections and romances.

> Beware of love in cyberspace.
> Oh, heed this warning do.
> When you fall in love on the internet,
> You fall in love with you.

This is to say, in talking to someone we do not know on the 'net, we are talking to ourselves. Any feelings that thus arise are self-generated and self-reflecting.

I told her about the sadness that had struck our family so suddenly just nine days before. Jean Darling, my eight-five-year-old stepmother of forty-four years, who had made my father so happy for so long, had died suddenly when an ulcerated vein in her leg burst. At 3 a.m., Dad got her into the ambulance but she was dead from loss of blood before it reached the hospital. I was acting in a play in Taupo, two hours' drive away, and got the news minutes before the final show, thankfully a matinee. I performed anyway and, as soon as the show was over, drove quite fast to Dad's place. By 7 p.m. I was with him, able to give comfort. I tucked him into bed that evening, with all the tenderness a son can give his shocked and stricken father.

I told Rose about my marital status, divorced after a two-year marriage twenty years before, and unencumbered of any attachments for the last three years. It's funny that we never talk about any of that because we covered it in our getting-to-know stage.

Two days into the whirlwind correspondence, I said I was, "Deeply trusting by nature, determined to retain the gullibility of youth well into my middle years–optimism they call it. So hi, Julia."

She replied, without any thought to what lay ahead. "Should I ever call you Darling, it would not only be a term of endearment but your name. Hmmm." She said she shared my sadness and asked me to bear with her, "As I try to move beyond my reticence about online meetings. You sound honest, fascinating, and very intelligent, all of which are very important to me. I'm glad to make your acquaintance too." And she noted that not many men would correspond with someone until they got a picture and she promised to send one. She was going off to church, to sing at two services, and the temperature in Ohio was 20F (6C). It was still only December 22.

By now she'd told me her birthday, which was six days before mine and I included in my next letter: "Thank you Lord for helping me meet Julia. And we were now signing our frequent emails, Fondly."

My email letter on Christmas Eve began with "Dearest JR," and included my phone number. We talked over the phone for the first time about 2 a.m. on my Christmas morning and I went back to bed, while her Christmas Eve continued.

Approaching the New Year, I wrote, "Without pre-empting life's fascinating turns too much, if you were to imagine yourself curled up beside a fire and safe in the knowledge of being loved, you would not be far wrong in imagining me as part of that scenario.".

Fast forward to the plane tickets I bought in February, my moving in the same month to take an editor-in-chief position at the South Taranaki newspaper I'd started at in 1980, and my arrival at Ohio's Akron-Canton airport at about 11 p.m. on Easter Thursday, April 8, 2004. I was in the front of the Air Trans plane from Atlanta but in the window seat. I asked the two women in the aisle and middle seats if they'd mind if I scrambled over them to get out first, because I was very excited to meet someone for the first time, at the arrivals gate.

It was love at first sight. Staring straight at this pretty blonde almost running toward me, everything fell into place, my destiny was right there and rightly ordered.

The next day, Good Friday, I took part in a "Cross Walk" around Willoughby, about an hour's drive north-east of Canton, and wore my monk's brown costume that is so much a part of my presentation. I was barefoot but had not expected a little snow that still lay on the ground. My lack of footwear amazed my fellow walkers, and as we went around Willoughby's central shopping area I was, in turn, amazed to find businesses open. On Good Friday? I had no idea that the United States does not keep this holiest of days as in New Zealand, where it is not only a public holiday but a day when trading of almost any kind is forbidden by law. New Zealand's Easter, with Monday also a public holiday, is a welcome four-day weekend, with very little business or shopping, either on Good Friday or Easter Monday. It's a respite from the constant demands of commerce and gets its origins from British custom.

Sport still goes on over Easter; the country's universities hold a traditional and very secular Easter Tournament in each of the main centers in turn. While most Americans think of New Zealand as "very beautiful" having seen the pictures taken on fine days, they often think of it as more secular than their country. Most realize the politics are quite left-of-center, compared with the U.S. And they know that free universal health care is offset by higher rates of income tax and long waiting lists for elective surgery. But it may have never occurred to them that, in New Zealand, the day of Jesus's crucifixion receives official state observance, as important as the birthday of the monarch.

The walk around Willoughby preceded a service at the local United Methodist church and I gave a twenty-minute performance of the Passion Story (Mark 14-16) and followed that at Rose's church on Easter Sunday, where she led a contemporary choir in a rock version of "Jesus Christ Is Risen Today!" That Sunday afternoon, I was kneeling on the floor of Rose's apartment, fixing an electrical plug and, as she walked past, I said with a smile, "Look, while I'm down here ..." She replied, "You know, I rather think I will."

Rose (by now we'd dropped the "Julia" through lack of use, even though she likes to be called Julia Rose by family in New Zealand) came to visit me for a week in June. Then we met for a week in October, in Honolulu, because it's halfway between Auckland and

Cleveland, and made plans for a wedding in Ohio the next Easter. We decided she would come to live in Hawera, the New Zealand town where I was the editor. And before that, Rose came to stay with me for a month over Christmas.

The hot Christmas Day I promised, the one where we would traditionally swim in the sea before a barbecue, never came. A cold snap put snow on top of our 2518m (8261 feet) mountain and a drizzly day meant a snug fire. She was right at home and after we married, she moved to New Zealand, intending to stay permanently.

Rose was soon hired as music director of the Anglican Cathedral, St Mary's, New Plymouth, about an hour's commute, and I was busy being a journalist again. St. Mark took some time off, though many people remembered my walk down the South Island and I was invited to a church in Christchurch, where the pastor was a friend of my mentor Jim Stuart.

It caused some discussion, even controversy, which the Christchurch pastor told me about a week later when he sent the agreed stipend. It seemed some of the congregation was intrigued by how I acted in the Garden of Gethsemane scene, with three disciples sleeping while Jesus prayed. In my interpretation, I mimed Jesus going to the sleeping Peter, hauling him up by his tunic front, shaking him, and loudly berating him. These were not the actions of a gentle Jesus, the parishioners thought. It provoked much discussion, which pleased me, and the vicar.

But thoughts of Rose and, of course, me, returning to the United States hung over us. After about a year, I realized we had to move when I saw Rose's sadness after a video call to her two grandchildren, then aged 5 and 3. The communication was a little incomplete and not very satisfactory. I decided we had to get her back home, even though it meant leaving the comparative paradise of New Zealand; compared, that is, with the large, beautiful, but deeply troubled United States of America.

The hardest part of the move was telling my 86-year-old father who had lived alone for two years since the death of his wife. He was going a little downhill from the great strength he once took for granted. It was late summer when we took him to lunch in a beautiful Hawke's Bay vineyard and told him of our plans. He asked what I would do for work, and I replied, "Do Mark."

He immediately changed the subject, an avoidance habit of his, and I knew he was not dealing well with the news, and realized he would never see me again. This was not his first loss by any means, but that did not make it easier. "Oh well, I don't believe in God," he said.

He was brought up strictly, and teetotally, Presbyterian. His atheism was only a recent acquisition and had begun when he started questioning important and basic tenets of the Christian faith, such as the virgin birth. He had decided that was preposterous, while still going regularly to his local Presbyterian church. The doubts multiplied, as doubts do, and he'd stopped going to church altogether about twenty years before. I watched and listened to his unbelief increasing over those years and I resolved I'd never let any doubt I might have keep me from the truth of the Way and the Life.

So, Dad knew that we planned to leave in two months and, although it's hard to admit, that news probably broke his heart. My phone calls to him, because we lived about four hours' drive away, met an increasingly weak and tired version of the once-booming voice. I feared he was fading fast and wrote to tell him we would visit on May 21, to say farewell.

I found that letter on his kitchen table. He had circled the date, which ironically became the day of his funeral. A few days before, he was not answering his phone. His sister Grace was anxious too and on May 18, I promised to let her know as soon as I heard from Dad. Instead, two young police officers arrived at the door and asked to come in, assuring me I'd done nothing wrong. No need to say more than, "It's Dad isn't it?"

His local police had gone around to the back of his house after neighborly concerns, they had not seen him for three days. The police saw him stretched out in the back bedroom, broke a window and entered, finding him clutching his heart, which had not beaten for a day or more.

He'd been alone for two and a half years since his wife Jean had died. Nobody should live alone and here was just another reason why. Of all the forms of accommodation, the single occupancy dwelling is the most impractical, for social and economic reasons Although it's increasingly popular to have people living in their own homes as long as they can, it's also increasingly dangerous to the health and wellbeing of participants. Living alone can be a form of solitary confinement, with few if any visitors and sporadic and unskilled care provided by irregular home health workers who are working for minimum wage, if that. Jesus's early followers had none of it and their communal living is noted in the book of Acts.

Prison Ministry

Once settled in Ohio, I began exploring the possibility of presenting Mark in prisons, while searching out churches willing to have me. I had already "done Mark," at least Mark 14-16, on my first visit to Ohio, at Willoughby in 2004. Now back in Canton, Ohio, I got busy. I hired the small theatre at the Canton Players Guild and set about selling tickets and giving them away, for two performances of Mark's Gospel. You can never tell enough people enough about these things. And even though I tried, I didn't (get the message out very well, judging by the paltry attendance). One church, that I visited to give away tickets, bore fruit, however.

I remember nothing about my first performance. It must have been immemorable. But the second produced an enduring contact in the portly form of Tom White, an agent for international organ impresario, Hector Oliviera. Tom was one of four in the audience, the others being his partner Ruth Ann, and two friends. They had taken advantage of the four tickets I left at their church in Canton.

Tom told me after the performance that their coming was no coincidence. "This was meant to be," he said, giving me knowing looks. I think he meant that I had blessed them with my recapturing of Mark's Gospel, taking the written Word and making it come alive. But I knew this was no coincidence because, without those kind words, I might have given up, as the sight of small audiences, several with their eyes down and reading. has tempted me to do so, before, and since.

I decided to visit prisons. I made a pamphlet and sent it off to as many chaplains as I could find on the registry of the Ohio Department of Corrections (ODOC). I did not ask for a donation as I expected that any mention of money would create an obstacle; they'd have to find a stipend for which they probably lacked a budget. So, this would be on my dime.

My first prison performance was in Grafton, in a snowstorm, on the plains that you find after an hour of driving west from Akron. As I checked in, I saw the men walking slowly, through the driving snow, from their outlying barracks to the central building where the chaplain was leading me. They looked like a scene from Dr. Zhivago, hunched over against increasingly driving snow, and I could almost hear the voices of the background male choir accompanying them. I settled into the performance well enough. It was a good warm-up (despite the snow) for a performance the next day at a church in Sandusky, on the shores of Lake Erie.

A few months later I was blessed with an uplifting experience, at the nearby Mansfield State Prison. I was going to perform there but I had to leave without sharing Mark's message, because a dinnertime fight in the cafeteria meant the inmates were in lockdown. So, my spirits lifted when a young man hailed me as I started to leave, "Godfrey!" he said.

"Well, that's close enough", I thought. "I'll take that", especially as he was so cheery. Godfrey is just a variation and, like my name, means "God's Peace."

"You saved my life," he said and explained that he'd been sitting and listening with the other prisoners at Grafton in the snow when suddenly he felt the sun coming out. It was still snowing outside but for him, a light came on.

"I decided right there I would do something with my life. I am going to get my G. E. D. and get a job so I can look after my wife and kid. Yes, the sun truly came out for me, the day you were there."

I promised I would get out to as many prisons as would have me, and many did; of course, they did. I worked for free. At each one, I thought about the prison farm inmates, four years before, who had all cried out "Yes" when Jesus said he was calling sinners to be his followers. I had a similar experience at the Belmont Correctional Institution, when the prisoners greeted the story of the empty tomb with a cheer. I had the young man, dressed in white and sitting on the tomb, say that they are looking for Jesus of Nazareth who was crucified and that He is not here, He is risen!. The prisoners responded with the same "Yes!" that I'd heard in New Zealand.

A middle-aged man approached me after one performance, saying he was being released soon and asking if he could get in touch with me on the outside. I think I'd told him I lived in Canton and he said that was not far from the halfway house he was going to. I gave him my number. A few weeks later I got a call and arranged to meet him at a McDonalds. I went to my pastor for advice and gained some incredible insights, not into how to comport myself with newly-released prisoners but into the psyche of the pastor, a man I was rapidly losing respect for. He gave me more "don'ts" than are in Leviticus, about how to keep my distance from this man, and he expressly forbade me to bring him to our church. As he wittered on, I had to keep reminding myself this was a servant of Jesus speaking. All regard for him drained away and I was relieved when Rose got an organ and piano playing job elsewhere and I had a good excuse to leave this dying church.

Entering each prison was just like the pre-flight security checks at every airport in the country. The scanners are the same but there is a stricter search of clothing, and of the accessories I planned to bring in. For the life of me, I cannot understand how drugs and other contraband can get into prisons. I admit that makes me naïve. but I retain a healthy cynicism nevertheless, I know the phrase is "healthy skepticism" but my version works well too.

My costume always got a thorough going over and I had to leave the rope, which went around my waist, behind with the guards. It is tied with the knots marking the monk's vows, of chastity, poverty, and obedience and acts as a belt. The guards could see it getting lost and the prisoners finding all sorts of uses for it. They could not risk it, so I left it with them and I always got it back.

Overall, I performed in a dozen ODOC prisons and wrote at least five times that many applications for grants. Most were ignored and those that came back offered nothing more than best wishes. One or two suggested I would have more success if I were a non-profit, registered with IRS. But without that, no money was forthcoming and I quietly let the prison ministry take a back seat and put the need to earn money to the fore.

By now I'd become noticed by the North East Ohio theatre community, well some of them, thanks to a wonderful production of *Equus,* directed by Bill Roudebush at Cleveland's Beck Center, in which I played the troubled boy's father. This was the play that gave me that deep insight into Jesus' call for us to "Be Ready" for his return, which I discussed on "Day Five" of the walk down the South Island.

The theatre community's interest was also sparked by my part in the annual joint theatres' auditions, for which I gave them a rousing Alfred Doolittle in a genuine cockney accent. I noticed several of the theatre heads sitting up as I entered, remembering me from *Equus.* After the audition, I got an offer from Magical Children's Theater in Barberton, not too far from our apartment in Canton. A few other offers came in, but too late, I'd accepted the first one. That was a principle of theatre etiquette I'd lived with all my life, to stay with my original commitment.

My time at "Magical" deserves a book of its own. Suffice it to say it was very happy, my first play was *Tuck Everlasting,* adapted from the 1975 classic by Natalie Babbitt, about a small pioneer family who had drunk from an enchanted spring and never aged from that moment. They spend the play trying to convince a young girl, who's also found the spring, not to drink. Much discussion about eternal life on earth concludes that it is infinitely better to be part of the cycle of life than to be stuck in one time, like the Tucks. It's an allegory, or a metaphor, or both, and although it's secular, it follows Christ's teaching, about using the gifts we have and using them wisely.

For a few years, I must admit, St. Mark took a back seat while I explored other theatre opportunities. I was still presenting Mark whenever I got invited but I often lacked the drive to push over the barriers of indifference and distrust that are, sadly, too common in established church circles. I decided that ninety minutes of Mark's gospel was too long for audiences used to spending just an hour in church and that not every Sunday neither. Many people asked me how long it took and were a little lacking in enthusiasm when I told them, "Ninety minutes". I didn't add that I left out Mark 7, quite a bit of Mark 11-12, and sometimes 13. Though in defense of Mark 13, when Jesus discusses eschatology, the quiet, simple recital of that chapter invariably gets such a still, fidgetless hearing, that you can hear the metaphorical pin drop.

Sermon on the Mount

As 2011 approached, I realized it was the 400th anniversary of the King James Bible. I learned the twenty-minute monologue in three months, longer than I thought I needed, but I was into my mid-sixties, and the learning conduits, through which words entered my brain, were starting to clog up, like my arteries. Only constant repetition would clear the channels now. So, for three months I worked on clearing them and was delighted with the result. It seemed ideal for churches who wanted a guest speaker.

It's still something I can perform with a few hours of revision. A few churches asked me to come as pulpit supply and I even presented it at a church's Christmas party. The King James Version is so well known, certainly something people of my generation grew up with, in a time before modern paraphrased versions became popular. It's hard to go past the majesty of such phrases as "Even Solomon in all his glory was not arrayed like one of these," "Whosoever shall smite thee on thy right cheek, turn to him the other also," or "Sufficient unto the day is the evil thereof." There is gravitas, or weight. in the King James, which sits well when delivered from memory.

After one performance, a young recent émigré from Russia told me she found the words harder to understand than usual. She thought she'd grasped English quite well in her three years in the United States, and she was almost chiding me when she said my presentation was harder to understand than usual. I told her the words were 400 years old and written by contemporaries of Shakespeare and Bacon, though I wasn't sure she was familiar with either. Nevertheless, the thought that I was saying the very words of Jesus and directly broadcasting his ideas sometimes awed me to an overwhelming extent. I still find it hard to take in.

Ireland and Ancestors

After my Sermon on the Mount presentation, people sometimes mentioned their wonder at listening to the greatest sermon ever preached, and I was pleased to hear them, but nothing compares with the thrill of saying Jesus's famous words, not just in the short bursts

Mark requires but for 20 minutes of sustained wisdom. I savor that now but I savor, with almost equal pride, the memory of presenting it in Ireland, in 2011.

Rose got me the gig, with as much ease as getting the attention of a U.S. church is difficult. We'd planned a two-week vacation with friends who were house-sitting, for a month, as part of their year-long working holiday in Europe. That's something young Kiwis do as part of gaining "Overseas Experience" or OE – but our friends were doing it as part of their midlife experience (ME). They were taking care of a house, or rather the pets in the house, while the owners took a long vacation.

The house was in Layton, a beach town just north of Dublin. Layton's beach is wide enough at low tide for the yearly Layton horse races, and the expansive sands, which seemed to stretch to the horizon, or to Wales, gave us plenty of long, fast walking in the two weeks of our stay.

Before we left Ohio, Rose contacted a Presbyterian Church in Drogheda (local pronunciation, "Droh- da"). Without a moment's pause, the vicar invited me to perform the Sermon on the Mount at the Sunday morning service and Mark's gospel in the evening. This was the Rev. John Woodside, who turned out to be tall and middle-aged and a huge fan of New Zealanders, on account of Kiwis having the most renowned rugby team in the world, the mighty All Blacks. His quick acceptance contrasted sharply with the oft-repeated ordeal of getting interest from a church in the United States. Chalk and cheese came to mind.

And so began St. Mark's adventure in Ireland, which had started with that quick acceptance, of saying "Yes" to the challenge without exploring it fully. It was stepping out in faith, something that has marked the many changes my life's taken. But this time it was the Rev. John Woodside who was stepping out in faith too. His trust and confidence in an unknown Kiwi went on to have much larger consequences for Rose and me, though we did not know it then.

At our first meeting, two days before the Sunday performances, John asked us if we'd heard of Willie John McBride. "Of course," we said, knowing he meant the legendary Irish lock forward and strong man of the 1960s and early '70s. Even Mike, not a great rugby follower, had heard of Willie John, a gentle name for an iconic giant of Irish, and world, rugby. John said the great man had been a close friend and clubmate at Ballymena in Northern Ireland. Because John was tall and fast, he played on the wing or center and said he'd often marked another legend of Irish rugby, Mike Gibson. Here was another player we knew well from our youth and were in as much awe of as Willie John.

We quickly realized John enjoyed talking about sports as much as religion, but his dedication to God was just as strong. In just a few years, he'd turned a struggling and crumbling church in the center of Drogheda, half and hour's drive north from Dublin, into such a viable community that a new church was being built for it, on the outskirts of town. This was Drogheda First Presbyterian, which was making many converts from other denominations as its numbers swelled, with John's guidance. He'd come late to the ministry, a former surveyor with three grown boys and Sandy, his charming wife.

The first presentation of the Sermon on the Mount, on Sunday morning coincided with an important rugby game, the semifinal of the 2011 Rugby World Cup being played in New Zealand. New Zealand played Australia and I watched the first half before John picked me up to go to his church.

Before the service we prayed together, and John said he realized it must be hard, with my mind half on the important game, when I was getting ready to perform. He admitted that, as a young man, he often drifted into thinking about his game on Saturday when he should have been praying on Sunday. I had to smile at that, such honesty, but I assured him I had no such problem. Part of being an actor was learning to "compartmentalize", and to shut out the world, just like having faith in God.

I reflected on the times I'd performed with worries on my mind, all weightier than whether the All Blacks could beat Australia, and all put aside with the same concentration that John and I now prayed for. It's the same concentration, and faith in God that I call on for writing this memoir, if truth be told. The All Blacks won so all was right with the world.

Two pew-packed performances followed, of Matthew 5-7 and then St. Mark, and the next day we drove to Northern Ireland to check out some ancestors. At this stage, I knew little of my Irish origins, apart from something a distant cousin in New Zealand had told me. This was our link to, among others, the Rev. Frederick Cassidy who brought his wife Martha and eight children, aged 21 to four, to New Zealand in 1872. Frederick Cassidy was my two-greats grandfather, and *his* father, the Rev. Mark Cassidy, had been the rector of St. Mark's in Newtownards, a town sixteen kilometers (ten miles) east of Belfast. So, to Newtownards we went.

Ireland is known for its green fields and amiable people, and for the short distances between places. Traveling to Newtownards, which the locals call "N'ards", was a piece of cake, with no border to cross, and the only problem, getting some local currency. We needed British pounds instead of the Euros of Ireland. The first ATM over the border solved that.

St. Mark's, Newtownards, was a revelation. Built of local limestone, it looked like a miniature cathedral but the welcome we got was as big as Westminster Abbey. Looking back over the years since, I still find it wonderful that my three-greats grandfather, Mark Cassidy, had been the driving force behind the creation of this beautiful building, in 1817.

The present rector, the Rev. Canon Chris Matchett, welcomed us and put aside his surprise at our unannounced visit. He took the time to show us around. He was new to the post, and as yet unsure of the church's history, but the verger, Ian, walked in and told us that the glass for a prominent window, which looked like a modern-art mosaic, came from windows in the church's former location, and is known to this day as the Cassidy Window, after my ancestors.

Ian was remarkable in his brand of military service. He could stay underwater, in a nuclear-powered (and nuclear-armed) submarine, for six months at a time. His fellow sailors would have had the same talent because that ability must be a gift. You can't teach such self-control. I wished I'd asked how the Royal Navy selected its long-stay-down submariners.

Ian knew a lot about the former site as well and told a fascinating, indeed awe-inspiring story, which I had a tangible link to. It was fascinating for colonials like us, coming from New Zealand with its mere 1,000 years of human history, and America, with its 400 years of

European settlement. St. Mark's previous site was Movilla, a hill above the town, first used in 544 A.D. when St. Finnian founded an abbey. It is believed that St. Columba was a student there. Vikings destroyed the abbey in a 9th Century raid but the ruins remained a place of veneration and pilgrimage for centuries. In 1244 the Benedictines built a priory on the site but that too fell into ruin, though a small chapel remained and worshippers still meet there on St Columba's Day, in June.

Since the 18th Century, a small Church of Ireland community met at Movilla regularly, in the chapel, which still stands though without a roof. The congregation grew and the church moved to the present site near the center of Newtownards, into the 1817 building. To our eyes, St. Mark's looked as fresh as paint, and Ian told us about the major renovations, restoration, and re-dedication just two years before.

As we looked around, and while Rose accepted the invitation to try out the organ, I got a sudden thought, to "Do Mark" here. I realized I could present Mark's gospel as part of the bicentennial celebrations in 2017, six years away. Canon Chris agreed at once, on our first meeting, without demur. It was the second time we'd been given a booking for St. Mark in Ireland and with typically Irish alacrity. So far in the future. it was easy to reach an agreement in principle. But time has a habit of passing and five years later I called to confirm a visit, in late August, with schools just going back.

Rose offered to play some hymns to break up the 90-minute presentation and in mid-August 2017, we traveled to Ireland, going first to England for a week. There we rented an airbnb in Canterbury, Kent, and made day trips to London, but also had a good look around the Cathedral, where I am sure I spoke briefly to the Dean, Canon Robert Willis, who later became so well-known for his daily YouTube broadcasts that were important for all Christians during the close, lockdown days of the covid pandemic.

Like all visitors to Canterbury Cathedral, we had been invited to take noon holy communion in the cathedral crypt and I was a little overwhelmed to find myself in a place my mother would have dearly loved to visit. After the service, a tall gentleman about my age, grey hair, etc., asked about us and our destination. He was respectfully interested to hear I was going to perform Mark's gospel in Northern Ireland and he wished me well, as I am sure he did all his guests, with the grace that shone so brightly in the broadcasts we came to love. Yes, my memory is sound. The more I think about it, I am sure it was him.

In our discussions with Canon Chris, about the visit and performance, I realized I simply could not ask for a fee. This was too special. Here was I, with the chance to present Mark's gospel in St. Mark's Newtownards, in honor of my ancestor, the Rev. Mark Cassidy M.A. (Trinity College Dublin). A unique Mark triple. So, in turn, Canon Chris would not let us pay for accommodation during our three-day stay, nor even pay for a meal. He found a beautiful apartment on the outskirts of town, down a narrow, hedge-lined, lane that had few places for two cars to pass and was thus typical of all of Ireland, yet so few vehicles on the road bore any marks of close encounters on those same country lanes. And Canon Chris hosted us for two evening meals and made sure a member of the congregation had us for the third.

We looked around Newtownards and found Bangor, a town to the north that formed a twenty-kilometer (thirteen-mile) triangle with Belfast, to the west of us. Ian, the verger and historian, told us Bangor once had a monastery, founded in the middle of the 6th century by St. Comgall of Antrim. At one time, 3,000 monks lived there in absolute self-sufficiency and solid devotion to God. Over the centuries the monastery grew to magnificence, becoming a great center of learning and defying, or surviving, Viking raids in the 9th century. The monastery still maintained some prominence until the 16th century dissolution of the monasteries.

Back in Newtownards, on the afternoon before the performance, I practiced part of St. Mark, to get a feel of the acoustics and the staging. I did not realize they were watching but I was happy to see how entranced both Ian and Canon Chris were in the rehearsal. I began the presentation in a corner of the church that, being too narrow, presented some staging difficulties. But since adaptability is my middle name, and no two venues are the same, I made it work as I had done so many times before.

I had only spoken a few verses and was up to John the Baptist baptizing Jesus when I felt a slight panic, a feeling that this was too big for me and I would not get through it. I'd never felt that before. I paused very briefly. For a short half-second. I gathered and quietly prayed for Jesus's help. And, in a moment, the audience would not have noticed, I carried on, refreshed and confident, all would be well. For less than a second, I had let the weight of the occasion overwhelm me and I stopped being in the moment, as they say. But the moment passed, and not by my doing.

I did not have time to think of it while performing but later I realized I'd been like Peter walking to Jesus on the water. A second's doubt and he was sinking, until Jesus gently rescued him. Mark's gospel skips over that part of Jesus's walk on water. In Mark the story has just Jesus walking on the water but the message is the same: With faith, we can do anything. And with faith, I stood in the hall of my ancestors and honored them, and God, because they expected no less.

My two-greats grandfather Rev. Fred Cassidy would have been in the church many times. He was one of the Rev. Mark's twelve children and one of three who followed their father into the church. Fred, my forebear, did not stay in the church long; just long enough to marry Martha Brown, a chambermaid half his thirty-four years. He was defrocked, not because of whom he married but how: He performed the ceremony himself. He continued to use the title Reverend, despite never practicing again. After farming in Donegal for almost twenty years, Fred and Martha and their eight children emigrated to New Zealand in 1872. The New Zealand Government wanted families with large numbers of girls, and Frederick's flock included three eligible women, including my great-grandmother Alice, who married the young Scots-born James Darling ten years later.

Knowing their history, I felt I was representing them in some way, and made the effort to visit the part of Donegal where Martha Brown grew up. It's named Bloody Foreland, not after some dreadfully gory battle but for the bright shining light the heather gives off at sunset, at certain times of the year. After the performance I talked to the audience, tucking into an excellent supper the church provided, and told a group of women, who'd come from the local Catholic Church, that we'd visited Bloody Foreland, about as far north in Ireland as you can go. They'd never heard of it and were quite taken aback to hear what they thought were "cuss" words in church.

The next day was Sunday and we'd booked on a train to Dublin that afternoon, before catching the plane back to the United States. But naturally, we first attended the main service in St. Mark's. The Irish hospitality was still in full swing after the late morning service. The whole church filed out past us, giving their blessings, with the oft-repeated wish, "Safe Home," which we heard them say at least 100 times. "Safe Home," is among the most delightful phrases coming from one of the most delightful countries.

And the hospitality was not done, nor was Canon Chris. Despite taking two services that morning, a modern one followed by a traditional one, he showed he intended to stay with us until our time in his precinct was over, until he'd seen us onto the train, two hours after the service. He should have been enjoying Sunday lunch with his family, but he followed our rental car to the drop-off at the Belfast airport and took us to the nearby train station. Instead of waving farewell, as we expected, this tall and generous man bought us lunch at the station buffet and waited with us, even though the express to Dublin was not due for an hour. We were a bit non-plussed at first but so happy to experience the above-and-beyond journey that the Irish take to practice what comes naturally to them, and to do no more than Jesus asked. Indeed commanded.

As we waited for the train, the laid-back Canon Chris amazed us with the depth of his courtesy, assuring us he'd nothing better to do, and we talked about the peace that Northern Ireland enjoyed now, and had done since the signing of the Good Friday agreement in 1998. This ended The Troubles, the sectarian violence that had been part of Northern Ireland's life since the 1970s. We saw no sign of it, in fact, quite the opposite. We saw a warm and happy country, but we weren't looking very hard. There is still mistrust and wariness of strangers, but we saw none of it, not in the Belfast region nor in Derry, where we also spent two nights. And after more than a decade in America, at that stage, I certainly knew what to look for.

That was August 2017, and the following February 2018, my home church, Christ Presbyterian in downtown Canton, where I am now one of the deacons, had me as part of the 2017-18 Concert Series, which usually features world-class musicians. I was incredibly honored to be chosen by the music director David Kienzle to present Mark as part of the prestigious programme. David was impressed that I'd gone to Ireland, to a church with links back to St Columba, and wanted to show some American appreciation of my Mark performance. It was one of the most well-attended concerts of the series that year. I and the 300 plus who filled the sanctuary found it unforgettable and I am delighted to have a recording of the evening, a live performance.

In the recording, David can be heard introducing the evening by teaching a simple part-song to a willing congregation, followed by readings and my presentation which is suitably interspersed with hymns. I repeated the last three chapters for the church's Good Friday service a few weeks later, again to a large audience, and decided that I would like to go out on a high, remembering the warmth of this large audience and hoping it would take away the cold of the disappointingly small audiences that I have encountered so often. That was my decision, but I also knew it didn't work like that. It has something to do with the sin of pride.

Like Jonah trying to escape his duty to God's calling, the desire to perform Mark's gospel persisted. I satisfied it when Rose began working as church visitation officer for a non-profit based in Bellevue, just south of Cedar Point, in 2019. Flat Rock is a residential care center for people with mental and physical disabilities and Rose's role was to raise awareness among churches in north-east Ohio. She took me along to spice up her presentation, which usually doubled as the sermon, with some excerpt from Mark.

We went to some very small churches, sometimes two on a Sunday morning because the pastor worked half-time at both. Once she did triple duty, a 9 a.m. service, a ten-kilometer (six-mile) drive, a 10.15 a.m. service, a fifteen-kilometer (nine-mile) drive, and an 11.15 a.m. service which the lay preacher had started before she arrived. This gave the thrice-way-stretched pastor a break and Rose was essentially "pulpit supply." At the first church Rose began and realised the church pianist had not arrived. Ever versatile, Rose stepped down from the pulpit and walked to the piano, played the hymn and returned to conducting the service. Such are the experiences that arise from a declining church population. We could ask those three (United Methodist) churches to merge, but we are forgetting the large distances between them. This is a problem for greater minds than mine.

In conclusion, I make a promise to keep "Doing Mark' while I can and live up to the advice of my father, Bruce Darling, who told me many, many times, "Never Give In." He repeated it so often I put it on a plaque to mark where his ashes are buried.

APPENDICES

The Timaru Herald of June 27, 2002, by Claire Allison

Walking with Geoffrey Darling you can't help but wish for a sturdy pair of trainers, like the ones that have carried him from Picton to Timaru and will carry him still further over the next couple of weeks.

Because shoes that are appropriate for a day in the office aren't quite so suitable for pounding up and down Timaru's hills, clutching a notebook and pen, and trying to interview the man over the roar of truck and trailer units on the highway. The hills are familiar to Geoffrey. He was born here and his father served at least ten years as the court register before his retirement in 1977.

This time he was here to perform Mark's Gospel as solo theatre – Mark's Midwinter Journey taking him to various communities throughout the South Island.

But the walk is the 53-year-old's own journey and despite many offers of rides, the odd snowfall, and a couple of days of rain, he's continuing with the Picton to Invercargill trek. Why walk? He says it's because he can and then expounds on how it's a traditional rite of passage for men his age to have a midlife crisis. but that not many would have the energy or the health to do this.

"It's nice to think I'll be able to get to the end and know that I have walked the whole way.

He had attempted a similar walk in the North Island but admits his training wasn't up to much and he had to pull out part-way through after his leg became infected. This time he did a lot more training – not just a couple of trots around the block.

He talks of the lies that road signs tell - of the sign that said Timaru was 10km away and a kilometre or so down the road the sign that said it was now 12kms away - a bit like Alice in Wonderland.

While many actors will rest before a solo performance, he's most likely to have walked a marathon. The longest day was Sunday – he set off from Dunsandel at 6 a.m. and walked to Rakaia. Then he walked from Rakaia to Ashburton and performed for an hour and a half that evening.

Offers to deliver his pack – at least 25kg – are gratefully received and he estimates he's probably carried that just a third of the way – leaving him free to admire snow on the mountains, sunrises and sunsets, to walk over bridges that span Canterbury's braided rivers and to play cricket. How?

You take the last digit of car rego numbers and keep adding up 7, 6, 3, etc. Comes a 0 – he's out. When the cars are few and far between it can be a long innings. One batter sat on 91 runs for quite some time before another vehicle came along … Would it be 0, or would it be 9? It was 9 and the batsman got his century.

Geoffrey has been offered the use of a hut in the Peel Forest and plans to spend a week there at the end of his journey, writing down his experiences and thoughts.

And since he started he's decided to add Stewart Island to the list of venues and perhaps perform at the pub there.

An actor first "back in the days when there wasn't much TV" Geoffrey spent most of his twenties in theatre, training in Adelaide, performing in a lot of regional theatres, and then going on his OE.

He trained as a journalist in 1980, because it seemed to be a more secure profession. But he muses on the fact that every newspaper he went to work for has closed down.

He's doing this series of solo performances as an actor but it is also about his faith which has grown since he started. He first performed St Mark's Gospel at Wellington's St Andrew's On The Terrace and has been developing it ever since.

Reprinted with permission from Stuff Ltd.

Hikoi of Hope
By Geoffrey Darling

The Anglican Church of New Zealand organized a "Hikoi of Hope" in September 1998. Hikoi means a march, a walk, or a demonstration in Maori. It turned out to be the largest march on Parliament in nearly a decade.

Participants began at both ends of the country and marched on Wellington. The marchers wanted change from the government to better citizens' lives. It was a march for social justice and a walk to bring hope to the dispossessed. It wanted the creation of real jobs, incomes, and benefits at a level that can bring people out of poverty, a trustworthy public health system, affordable housing, and accessible and affordable education.

It sprang from the May meeting of the General Synod for the Anglican Church in Aotearoa New Zealand and Polynesia. A session that began with concerns over welfare benefit changes escalated into a major debate about poverty and then the decision to start the Hikoi of Hope.

From September 1, people began walking for change, with many threads of the hikoi led by heads of all churches. People walked from twelve regions, going all the way, which some undertook, or handing over the impetus of the hikoi at the next town. In Whanganui, 200 kilometers (120 miles) from Wellington, four people walkers arrived from further 'upstream', and 500 locals walked down the main street with them. A forum, speeches, and a church service ensued and the next day about twenty walked on south to Bulls. Such scenes were repeated throughout the country and the stories told were gathered and presented to the government. At their core was concern that New Zealand had a growing poor underclass and a widening gap to the rich elite. Given New Zealander's strong egalitarianism, this was a major concern.

Small towns, where the pain of social change is felt most, showed a lot of support to the estimated 30,000 New Zealanders who took part. Larger towns were a bit nervous, at the concept of protest in general, while the cities showed either indifference or total support.

Five years later, in 2004, at an address in Christchurch Cathedral, Prime Minister Helen Clark said the Anglican Church was not a political movement. "It is a religious community with a strong spiritual and ethical foundation. It is based in communities throughout the land. It can perceive what the concerns of communities might be, and reflect on how they might be represented and addressed.

"For me, the Hikoi of Hope had enormous symbolism, which transcended even its advocacy of the core planks of a decent life for all New Zealanders. That symbolism lay in the sense of social solidarity which it engendered."

The Prime Minister used her address to highlight her Government's success in implementing changes sought by the hikoi.

"In December 1999, we started on a journey of rebuilding opportunity and security and that sense of a fair go which most New Zealanders value so highly. Twelve weeks of paid parental leave came into law in 2002. Compared to when the Hikoi of Hope came to Parliament in late 1998, over 200,000 more New Zealanders are working now. That is spectacular progress, and it's been felt across our communities. I believe that our government, over these past four and a half years, has responded comprehensively to the call of the Hikoi of Hope for action. I don't pretend that the job is done, but I know that it is well underway and that our will to continue on the journey is strong, said Prime Minister Clark.

Kemra Bank

Although Kemra Bank and Mayfield were bought simultaneously, the Smaill and Darling families both lived for some months on Kemra Bank before a house was built for the Smaills on Mayfield. Our thanks are due in large measure to William Smaill who, in the 1920s, when he was over 70-years- old, sat down and wrote a volume of reminiscences which has been of the greatest value, not only for the light it sheds on the settlement of these two farms but for the information it brings to us about other island families of the time.

Arriving in Otago on the "Strathallan" on January 8, 1858, the two Edinburgh families settled for a time at Anderson's Bay. William Smaill lists the members of these families – grandmother (mother's mother),

Aunty Fanny (father's sister), Andrew and Christina Smaill, both aged 43, who were the parents of Agnes (14 years), Andrew (12), James (10), William (8), Robert (7), John, and Tom the baby; John (46) and Janet (43) Darling and their children Jeannie (12), James(10), Lizzie, Robert and Mary. Ella Darling, born at Anderson's Bay, raised the Darling total to 8, the whole party to 19.

Since both fathers had been grocers in Edinburgh, they decided to seek farm work for a short time in the new country before selecting land for themselves. Harvest work was offering at James MacAndrew's on the Peninsula, so off went the two fathers, with Andrew and sometimes Aggie, every morning, walking back wearily at night after their unaccustomed exercise, until the harvest had been completed. Meanwhile, from James MacAndrew, the two men were gathering information concerning the location of likely farms; so when they started for the Clutha early one morning in mail-carrier Jock Graham's trap, they had some knowledge of the settlers on whom they were to call for advice, and of the sections yet unclaimed.

Reaching the Clutha ferry, Andrew Smaill and John Darling turned and followed the riverbank down to "Mt. Coo-ey" where they were probably crossed by William Willocks, for he was apparently the first Islander they met. On they went, down to the home of the three Smith brothers. William, Peter and Joseph. at The Bush, and Maitlands at Pen-y-dre, then crossed over to Myres to meet Pillans and Ferguson, and down to Woodside to see W. A. Mosley.

But still no land. All the best sections seemed to have been taken up, and as yet they had met no-one willing to sell. "Try the Coast?" someone suggested, "None of the Coast sections have been bought yet."

They tried the Coast. From Davidson's at The Gask they were piloted to Lovell's home at Kaitangata Creek; from here the pair started out up Kaitangata Hill on their own, through rank growth with only wild pig tracks, since there were few cattle there yet. The idea was to travel along the Wangaloa coastline to the river, then up the riverbank and so back to Lovell's before dark; but the rank growth of flax, toitoi, and fern made this impossible. As darkness set in they reached Summerhill; sat down, had a snack and discussed the situation.

Below them in the gloom lay the great river, snaking round and out to sea far along the sandspit. All at once they noticed a light. It looked like a house light, across the river. Well, anything was better than camping out in this unknown county with only wild pigs for company; so the two men scrambled down somehow through the rough growth and made for the riverbank opposite the light, where Andrew coo-eed lustily till he noticed a boat putting off from the far bank.

Mrs Willie Mitchell was alone in the small, rough cottage with its calico windows. Her husband was away up to the Ferry for stores, and would not be back till the morrow. On hearing the coo-ee she was non-plussed, until she thought of the party of Maoris camped along on the point, where they were fishing.

The Maoris did not like moving in the dark, but somehow she persuaded several of the party to cross the river and bring over the strangers. As the two men came up the riverbank to the light from the open doorway, Mrs Mitchell gasped, then cried out: "Mr Smaill, where have you come from?" Andrew started, peered at the woman's face in the dim lights, and exclaimed, "Katie Lindsay, how are you here!" For Katie Lindsay had been one of his customers in his grocery store in Edinburgh. How they talked"

"Land?" said Willie Mitchell on his return next day. "Yes, a couple of hundred acres of good land and more later if you want it. No, I don't understand why it's not been taken up. Yes, it's on the waterway not far from the mouth. Good land too, a bit peaty but it'll grow anything."

Acting on their host's advice they came to the two clearings above the Balloon, looked around at the most impenetrable thicket that clothed nearly the entire length of the riverbank, but having heard Willie Mitchell's talk of the crops of potatoes the Maori had been known to take off these clearings, they decided to apply for this land. Since the sections were adjacent, the men drew lots and to his evident satisfaction, John Darling drew the more attractive section, containing a Maori whare and a larger clearing. Returning to Dunedin they lodged their applications for the sections which were granted on February 15, 1858. They named their farms quite early. The name Kemra Bank was being used as early as 1863. No trace can now be found of the origin of its name. It is unknown in survey gazetteers in Scotland or in Edinburgh directories. Descendants of the Darling family know nothing of the origin of this name, given by John Darling and his wife to their Inch Clutha farm.

Having arranged for the baggage and the household effects of the two families to be brought round from Dunedin on the coastal vessel "The Spec", the two men next arranged for the transport of the whole party overland by bullock dray, after which Andrew Smaill again set off for the Clutha to prepare for the coming of the group. On the day of their departure from Anderson's Bay, all were up with the birds; bedding and utensils were packed and everything was in readiness very early for the expected dray. But no dray. They waited and waited. The vehicle finally turned up and was packed high with the gear.

It was after midday before they could get on their way and with the difficult country of that period to traverse, there was no hope of reaching their objective, Scrogg's Creek (now Allanton) that night. Indeed they could travel no further than Lookout Point, where they spent the night; most of the children having to walk as any available room on the dray must be reserved by the mothers and their infants.

Not till nearly midday next day did they arrive at Scrogg's Creek where Antonio Joseph met them, as arranged, with his boat. What delight the youngsters found in their sail "on a beautiful river with beautiful banks on either side, the water pure and clear". It was ten years before William Smaill passed that way again and in that time what a change had been wrought, "Not in the way of beautifying, "says William bitterly.

Next day they sailed the length of Lake Waihola, transferred to another bullock dray at the southern end of the lake, and reached Tokomairiro just after dark.They spent the night in James Smith's barn. The last stage was out into the unknown, with no human habitation for the 20 miles from Tokomairiro and the Clutha, which they reached at dusk, again with most of the family walking ahead or beside the dray. In the growing darkness the last weary trudge down to the river bank, to Smith's Bush, seemed endless but at last they arrived.

The Smith brothers, comparative newcomers themselves, had been busy that day harvesting their wheat with the help of Willie Aitchison, James Wright and Thomas Marsh, all of whom were living at Myres at the time. Turning not a hair at this invasion by an army of 18-strong, the Smiths prepared a meal, after which the three workers rowed six of the party across to Myres to spend not only the night but a day or two extra to recover from their journey.

For the last stage of their trip they were packed into a four-ton boat, which with the three Smiths and four workers for crew, carried them rapidly down the Matau to Kemra Bank. They were overcome by the beauty of the river and its environs. "Every bend," says Major Smaill, "was a new beauty."

As they swung round the Mayfield bend the full view of the Kaitangata Range burst upon them, thickly clad in bush and mirrored in the clear water of the river on this beautiful autumn morning. Soon they were round the bend and stepping onto Kemra Bank at a point where a Maori whare stood in a clearing.

They were greeted by Andrew Smaill and young Andrew who had prepared a meal for them to eat amid confusion and merry chatter and sense of bewilderment and yet thankfulness that they were at last on their own land. The meal was set on a makeshift table in the whare which measured about 18ft x 12ft. This one small room was to eat and sleep at least 19 people for some weeks until a simple house had been built by the Darlings after which the Smaill family continued to use it until their own first house was built at Mayfield. Hardly had they farewelled the boat and the crew on their return journey upriver, and attempted to settle in, than evening fell; and after an evening meal of sorts, the whole company joined in family worship, psalm, chapter, and prayer, according to the custom of their generation. Indeed the families observed this practice into the following generations.

Reprinted from *The Inch* by Alma Rutherford by kind permission of her family.

BIBLIOGRAPHY

Branscomb, Harvie B. *The Gospel of St. Mark*. Hodder and Stoughton. 1938

The Inch: The Story of Stirling and Inch Clutha by Alma M.Rutherford, The Clutha Leader Print, 1958,

ABOUT THE AUTHOR

GEOFFREY DARLING is a New Zealand actor and journalist, now happily settled in Ohio with his wife Rose, a church musician. After graduating from Rotorua Boys' High School in 1966, he set out to cram as much into his life as possible. That included time as a bus tour guide, covering almost all of New Zealand before he was 21, an acting student in Adelaide, a Kiwi Abroad in London, a cave guide on his return to New Zealand, and an actor in regional professional theatres. He returned to formal study at thirty, graduating from the Wellington Poly. Journalism School with the Feature Writing Prize in 1980. In twenty-five years in newspapers, he worked in provincial dailies, edited three community newspapers and was a press ssecretary in Parliament. All in the North Island.

Printed in the United States
by Baker & Taylor Publisher Services